STANDARDS IN PRACTICE GRADES 9–12

STANDARDS IN PRACTICE GRADES 9–12

PETER SMAGORINSKY

National Council of Teachers of English

1111 W. Kenyon Road, Urbana, Illinois

61801–1096

Manuscript Editor: Kurt Kessinger
Production Editor: Michelle Sanden Johlas
Cover and Interior Design: R. Maul
Cover Photograph: Thompson-McClellan Photography
Interior Photographs: Lori B. Gillman, p. 8; Anne Sullivan, p. 26;
NCTE, pp. 47, 71, 109

NCTE Stock Number 46953-3050

Library of Congress Cataloging-in-Publication Data
Smagorinsky, Peter.
    Standards in practice, grades 9–12 / Peter Smagorinsky.
        p. cm.
    Includes bibliographical references.
    ISBN 0-8141-4695-3
    1. Language arts (Secondary)–United States.   2. Language arts
(Secondary)–Standards–United States.   I. Title.
    LB1631.S52   1996
    428'.0071'2–dc20   95-49757

FOREWORD

This book is one of four in the NCTE Standards in Practice series. The idea for this series grew out of requests from many teachers around the country who participated in the development of the NCTE/IRA standards and who asked if we could publish a book or a series of books that would illustrate what the standards might look like in actual classrooms at different grade levels.

This request was both inviting and challenging. Because one of the main goals of NCTE is to support classroom teachers, providing a series of books that would help define the standards seemed like the sort of thing we should do—and it is the type of thing, we like to think, we do quite well. At the same time, there were many challenges in developing these books. We wondered: Could we do it? What might these books look like? What standards would we use? How important would uniformity and consistency be among the books in the series?

The four authors and I spent time exploring these questions and it soon became evident that the development of this series was, perhaps, both simpler and even more important than we had originally thought. We decided that if we asked English language arts teachers who were doing interesting and challenging work in their classrooms to reflect in writing on their practices and to tell us their stories, the standards would be there, already at work in students' learning. After all, the English language arts standards did emerge from those practices that our membership and the IRA membership said they valued most. The standards do not stand above and apart from the practices of actual classroom teachers, or dictate to them—rather they represent what those teachers and the many others involved in English language arts education agree is the best and most productive current thinking about teaching and learning. We also decided that each book in the series did not have to follow the same generic format. What each book should do instead is tell its own story and use the format that best fits and supports the story or stories being told.

All of us agreed that we wanted the books in this series to be stories or rich illustrations of classroom practice. Stories, we thought, would allow the writers to capture the rich and complex activities of teaching and learning and, in addition, would illustrate the interconnectedness of the English language arts and of the standards themselves. We also wanted our readers to see how teachers create contexts as well as learning experiences. We thought it was important for the readers to experience both the struggles *and* the successes teachers and students encounter. And we hoped that the stories would make explicit the importance of the teacher as researcher. We believe the standards are dynamic in nature and will change and improve only if teachers actively and deliberately interrogate their own practice—learning and growing from their professional and classroom experiences.

In these four books we meet caring teachers who meet all our most challenging criteria for teaching and learning. They are women and men who think deeply about the quality of life and intellectual growth they provide for their students. Some of the teachers we meet in the series are new to the profession and are trying out ideas for the first time. Others have been teaching for many years but, as always, are reflecting on and questioning some of their practices, and in their stories we see them making changes. All of them, whether they are teaching five-year-olds or eighteen-year-olds, whether they themselves have been teaching for five or for eighteen or more years, put students' learning at the center of their curricula and engage their students in challenging, authentic experiences. By presenting an array of classroom portraits, these volumes clearly show that standards are always present in good practice and that there is no one way for the standards to be realized.

I want to commend the teachers and students who are featured in this series and the writers who told their stories. They have opened their classrooms to us and let us look in, and, in so doing, they have enriched our understandings of what matters most in the English language arts.

–Karen Smith
Associate Executive Director
National Council of Teachers of English

CONTENTS

NCTE/IRA
STANDARDS FOR THE ENGLISH LANGUAGE ARTS

The vision guiding these standards is that all students must have the opportunities and resources to develop the language skills they need to pursue life's goals and to participate fully as informed, productive members of society. These standards assume that literacy growth begins before children enter school as they experience and experiment with literacy activities–reading and writing, and associating spoken words with their graphic representations. Recognizing this fact, these standards encourage the development of curriculum and instruction that makes productive use of the emerging literacy abilities that children bring to school. Furthermore, the standards provide ample room for the innovation and creativity essential to teaching and learning. They are not prescriptions for particular curriculum or instruction.

Although we present these standards as a list, we want to emphasize that they are not distinct and separable; they are, in fact, interrelated and should be considered as a whole.

1. Students read a wide range of print and nonprint texts to build an understanding of texts, of themselves, and of the cultures of the United States and the world; to acquire new information; to respond to the needs and demands of society and the workplace; and for personal fulfillment. Among these texts are fiction and nonfiction, classic and contemporary works.

2. Students read a wide range of literature from many periods in many genres to build an understanding of the many dimensions (e.g., philosophical, ethical, aesthetic) of human experience.

3. Students apply a wide range of strategies to comprehend, interpret, evaluate, and appreciate texts. They draw on their prior experience, their interactions with other readers and writers, their knowledge of word meaning and other texts, their word identification strategies, and their understanding of textual features (e.g., sound-letter correspondence, sentence structure, context, graphics).

4. Students adjust their use of spoken, written, and visual language (e.g., conventions, style, vocabulary) to communicate effectively with a variety of audiences and for different purposes.

5. Students employ a wide range of strategies as they write and use different writing process elements appropriately to communicate with different audiences for a variety of purposes.

6. Students apply knowledge of language structure, language conventions (e.g., spelling and punctuation), media techniques, figurative language, and genre to create, critique, and discuss print and nonprint texts.

7. Students conduct research on issues and interests by generating ideas and questions, and by posing problems. They gather, evaluate, and synthesize data from a variety of sources (e.g., print and nonprint texts, artifacts, people) to communicate their discoveries in ways that suit their purpose and audience.

8. Students use a variety of technological and informational resources (e.g., libraries, databases, computer networks, video) to gather and synthesize information and to create and communicate knowledge.

9. Students develop an understanding of and respect for diversity in language use, patterns, and dialects across cultures, ethnic groups, geographic regions, and social roles.

10. Students whose first language is not English make use of their first language to develop competency in the English language arts and to develop understanding of content across the curriculum.

11. Students participate as knowledgeable, reflective, creative, and critical members of a variety of literacy communities.

12. Students use spoken, written, and visual language to accomplish their own purposes (e.g., for learning, enjoyment, persuasion, and the exchange of information).

INTRODUCTION

Most of the adventures recorded in this book really occurred; one or two were experiences of my own, the rest those of boys who were schoolmates of mine. Huck Finn is drawn from life; Tom Sawyer also, but not from an individual—he is a combination of the characteristics of three boys whom I knew, and therefore belongs to the composite order of architecture.

... Although my book is intended mainly for the entertainment of boys and girls, I hope it will not be shunned by men and women on that account, for part of my plan has been to try to pleasantly remind adults of what they once were themselves, and of how they felt and thought and talked, and what queer enterprises they sometimes engaged in.

Mark Twain, *Preface to* The Adventures of Tom Sawyer

With some slight revision, Twain's preface to *Tom Sawyer* could easily describe what I have tried to do in this addendum to the NCTE/IRA standards. I am illustrating the NCTE/IRA standards in practice through a set of five vignettes of teachers and students in action. These stories are, by most definitions of the term, fictions; that is, what I relate in the narratives did not literally occur in specific classrooms. Rather, they are composites of teaching and learning based on my experiences with schools since I started out as a substitute teacher in central New Jersey in 1975—or perhaps since 1966, my first year as a high school student in northern Virginia. They are thus fictions in the sense that *Tom Sawyer* is a fiction; or to use a more contemporary analogy, they are fictions in the manner of Theodore Sizer's *Horace's Compromise*. By this I mean that the stories I present are not tied to a specific reality but are based on many realities.

Among my main goals in creating these narratives is to show how teaching is not a generic process of the sort typically described in publications about teaching. Frequently, educational publications represent teaching as a process that can be exported wholesale from one teaching situation to the next. In this set of narratives I try to reveal teaching and learning as situated in settings that present specific constraints and potentials for teachers and students. Courtney Cazden has referred to learning as being "nested" in contexts that include the schools, communities, states, and nations that provide the conditions that help shape how teaching and learning unfold. Commercial textbooks and statewide curricula often assume that teaching is a one-size-fits-all proposition; that the discussion and homework questions prescribed in the teacher's manual are the best questions to ask about literature no matter who is teaching or learning. I believe instead that teachers take into account who and where the learners are; that a teacher in a large, comprehensive, multiethnic urban high school does not make the same decisions about implementing a curriculum as does the teacher in an affluent, homogeneous suburban school or the teacher in a small rural community where the students—and often the teachers and administrators—work the family farm before and after school. I have tried in these vignettes to show how the learning context provides the resources, value systems, and other conditions that influence the process of education. I have thus created settings for the stories that are not amenable to stock responses from teachers.

The NCTE/IRA standards make an effort to identify what students should know. I have tried to illustrate that what students learn in school is a consequence of what students know from cultural experiences outside school. Students come to school with a great deal of knowledge about human relations, economics, speech conventions, value systems, cultural practices, authority structures, and other aspects of social life often overlooked in policymaking about education. As Twain notes in his preface to *Tom Sawyer*, adults (including educators) often forget what childhood is like. Through these narratives I hope to illustrate teachers who are in tune with their students and build instruction on what they bring to school. This is *not* to say that the vignettes depict schooling as formal narcissism, as some critics argue is the case with learner-centered schooling. Rather, they show teachers who capitalize on students' strengths to help them grow into more complex, knowledgeable, and literate people. The curriculum thus becomes a means rather than an end; it is a tool that students use to change on their way toward becoming better informed, more capable citizens.

Though each vignette is a sort of fiction, all are tied to real situations. "Red Ribbon Week" draws its setting from an oil town in Oklahoma that I've worked with, although for this narrative I've moved it to the West Coast where many similar towns exist. The town where I've situated this story is intended to represent the plight of many communities whose stability is tied to the presence of a single employer, such as an oil refinery, military base, factory, or other large enterprise or service. The substance of the instruction is borrowed loosely from curriculum developed by Kathy Woods of West Mid-High in Norman, Oklahoma, during her master's degree program at the University of Oklahoma. This I have combined with materials from my many years of teaching high school sophomores in the Chicago suburbs. "Perspectives on *Huckleberry Finn*" is a very personal story, based on my teaching experiences in Illinois in the 1980s. The story I tell here weaves together many classroom experiences I had discussing *Huckleberry Finn* with multiracial high school juniors. "Tales of the Prairie" is not based on any particular school or community, but rather is a mosaic drawn from small schools in rural Oklahoma that I've visited, or communities I've come to know through the literacy autobiographies written by my preservice and graduate students at the University of Oklahoma who grew up in small farming and ranching towns. Additional details for this story are derived from research I've done in a high school agriculture class in central Oklahoma.

"The Color of the Curriculum" draws heavily from two sources: a teacher-research master's thesis written by Darlene Brown at the University of Oklahoma, and the teacher-research doctoral thesis of Carol Lee conducted at the University of Chicago and later published as an NCTE Research Report, both of which concern the teaching of *The Color Purple*, although with vastly different student populations. The examples of student writing and dialogue that I include are adapted from these sources; "Flossie and the Fox" is a story I've read with my own young children. "Coming to America" borrows its premise from a videotape of Laura Schiller's teaching that I watched while working on the National Board for Professional Teaching Standards assessment project. I've situated this narrative in an urban school that is a composite of the twenty-five or so schools in which I substitute taught in Chicago during the early 1980s while completing my doctoral course work. By changing the locale I had to adjust her practice to the teaching and learning conditions of the new setting.

I present a number of examples of student writing and student discussion in these vignettes, none of which is a strict transcription from an actual classroom. But each one has a basis in real student work, at times from my own teaching in Illinois and at times from the classes of teachers I know in central Oklahoma. "Red Ribbon Week," for instance, includes a small-group discussion that is adapted from tapes I recorded when researching my own high school teaching in 1989. Some of the student writing I've included, such as that in "The Color of the Curriculum," is based on the work of students from the teacher-research studies I drew on to create the narratives. "Perspectives on *Huckleberry Finn*" includes discussion excerpts that are based on classroom conversations I had with students in my own high school English classes. The vignettes therefore are not the verbatim products of case studies of students and teachers, but composites of what students have produced in response to such instruction. Even though the stories I tell are fictions of a type, I hope that they relate some truth about classrooms.

Writing these narratives has at times been very difficult, even agonizing for me. In several of the narratives I represent the complexities of teaching in multiracial communities. Depicting the experiences of people from cultures other than my own has been a vexing task, one that has caused me a great deal of uneasiness. I, like most Americans, come from a mixed-culture background myself: My father is the son of Byelorussian Jews who immigrated to New York around the time of World War I; my mother is of German and Irish descent and grew up Catholic in Brooklyn. Until I was in the seventh grade I attended racially segregated schools in Virginia; in addition, we were the only non-Protestant family in the neighborhood where I grew up, clearly marked as outsiders by our exotic name, appearance, and speech. These experiences have impressed on me the difficulties people have in seeing life from another person's perspective. I know how hard it is to understand the cultural experiences of other people; through writing these narratives I now know that it is even more difficult to represent them in story. In my research for this project, I came across scathing critiques by Native American authors Leslie Marmon Silko and Geary Hobson of white writers who have attempted to depict fictional Native American characters. I also read Lisa Delpit's views on the difficulties well-intentioned white teachers have understanding the cultural backgrounds of minority students. Needless to say, their views did not quiet my own doubts about my ability to accurately describe the experiences of culturally diverse students; I have worried mightily that in trying to do the right thing I have done many wrong things.

To help me create depictions of life from the viewpoint of a variety of cultures so that they resonate with reality, I have asked friends from many and diverse backgrounds to critique what I have written. I hope that their feedback has helped me avoid perpetuating old stereotypes and creating new ones. Undoubtedly my representation of the experiences of diverse students will not satisfy everyone. Yet I strongly believe that it would be impossible and irresponsible for me to describe schooling at the close of the twentieth century and only describe classrooms that include students whose values, outlooks, and appearance are similar to mine.

The problem of representing other cultures becomes acute when attempting to depict some communities as they actually are, inequities and all. Some of the communities I describe are culturally diverse in ways that produce tensions and conflicts among townspeople. In "Perspectives on *Huckleberry Finn*," for instance, there is great disagreement among parents, students, and teachers of the community on the ways in which the cultural diversity of the citizens should affect the values of schooling. In my effort to describe such communities I have included race-based distinctions and conflicts because I think they reveal the ways in which school structures can manifest the class- and race-based inequities of the communities that they serve. By placing minority students in disadvantaged or oppositional positions, however, I run the risk of being mistakenly interpreted as supporting such social structures and of creating a representation that reinforces negative images of society. My purpose is to illustrate the tensions that characterize many American communities and their consequences in the classroom. I have taught in such communities and know that even schools whose mission includes the celebration of diversity—of race, ethnicity, religion, sexual orientation, social class, and other factors—often have difficulty in gaining broad consensus on that mission or realizing their stated goals in practice.

If I were to fictionalize the narratives so that they falsely painted all multicultural classrooms as equitable and harmonious, I would be dodging one of the most perplexing aspects of teaching and learning in diverse communities. America, in spite of the equalities guaranteed in its Constitution, is a nation of personal and structural inequities that become embodied in educational practices. Overlooking these inequities would make this book a weak effort to illustrate educational standards in practice, particularly at a time when issues of diversity are so important in considering the process and product of education. Including them, on the other hand, has created for me dilemmas that I can only hope I've presented in a way that readers will find satisfactory. It's much easier to *say* that we should celebrate diversity than to actually *do* it in our practice, even if we assume that all or most members of a community agree on multiculturalism as a goal. As I've found in writing these narratives, it's equally difficult to present complex diversity issues in story form.

In addition to agonizing over cultural issues of race, ethnicity, and social class, I've also included facts of life for many teachers and students that are, to say the least, of questionable influence in creating equitable educational environments. The teachers in these narratives often teach in schools that use tracking, a practice that NCTE has officially opposed in one of its resolutions. The teachers also work in states that mandate exams that teachers are pressured to prepare students for, teach in communities where test scores are used to calibrate the effectiveness of the schools and the value of real estate, and teach in departments where seniority reigns and creates a class system within the faculty. In some of the schools I describe the teachers have little authority in decision making, and students less. By representing these very real teaching conditions, I do not endorse them. I simply want to show classrooms as they are, fully nested within contexts great and small, sublime and ridiculous, that influence teachers' and students' efforts to develop appropriate literacies. Good teachers do not transcend such conditions, but operate within their constraints.

Following each narrative is a set of reference lists pertinent to the issues addressed. I hope that teachers find these resources useful should they want to consult additional sources to further consider the issues raised in the stories. Included are a variety of tools: books and articles to read, networks to develop, journals to subscribe to, and e-mail discussions to participate in. Of course, none of these lists is comprehensive, and undoubtedly each could be supplemented with additional resources; in particular, e-mail and World Wide Web resources should expand rapidly in the next few years beyond what I've described here. (The following e-mail address will provide you with a comprehensive listing of electronic-mail discussion networks: <listserv@bitnic.bitnet>. To this address, send a message consisting of a single word: *global*.) I hope that they can at least provide a start for teachers looking for ideas to consider in their decision making.

Many friends and colleagues have read and responded to drafts of this manuscript along the way. I owe great thanks to Nancie Atwell, Mary Belgarde, Darlene Brown, Helen Burgess, Linda Crafton, Lolita Green, Kris Gutierrez, Dan Heller, Betty Houser, Carol Lee, Cindy O'Donnell-Allen, Patty Reed, Marty Sierra-Perry, Janet Smith, Karen Smith, Joan Steiner, Lynda Thompson, and Jeff Wilhelm for taking time away from their own work to provide thoughtful critiques and suggestions that strongly influenced the development of the narratives. In particular I'd like to thank Karen Smith for putting together this project and coordinating it. These friends and colleagues have helped me to see problems with my original conception of these vignettes and have helped me see better ways to present them.

Finally, I owe great thanks to my family for allowing me the time to work on this project. As always, they both tolerate and inspire my work. I hope that as my children go through school they will benefit from the various standards projects currently under way to improve learning and teaching in our classrooms.

DEDICATION

Dedicated to the students
in the hopes that our efforts to develop standards
will help them see ways to develop their own

CHAPTER ONE

RED RIBBON WEEK

Pacific Hills was a medium-sized town on the West Coast whose economy rested precariously on the stability of the oil refinery located at the edge of town. The refinery provided employment for many of the town's residents and also generated much subsidiary employment. Businesses in town tended to thrive when the plant operated at full capacity, and floundered or folded during the chronic layoffs. Events halfway across the world had strong ripple effects on Pacific Hills. Conflict in the Mideast might cause changes in domestic oil supply and demand that would affect the refinery's employment needs, and thus the economy of the town. Pacific Hills's population was in a constant state of flux, burgeoning during periods of peak oil production and then dropping during lay-offs when refinery workers moved to other towns to find available work. When the oil workers left town, business would drop off elsewhere and cause layoffs in department stores, restaurants, and other businesses. Life in Pacific Hills was characterized by uncertainty and adaptability as people adjusted to the economy's fickle moods.

The school system, like every other institution in town, was gripped by apprehension. With every shift in the size of the refinery's workforce came shifts in the size of the student body. On a moment's notice the factory might lay off several hundred workers, many of whom would immediately leave town in search of other jobs, often taking their families with them and changing the population of the schools. The school system, which was always strapped for money, always had a number of teachers "on the bubble," ready to receive notices of reductions in force when student enrollment dropped. While senior faculty members had job security, newer teachers were always anxious about their future in the district. The lack of stability in both the student body and the faculty led to a sense of vulnerability in the school as a whole.

The school's administration followed a top-down model of decision making. Too many faculty members had uncertain futures in the district for the teachers to provide an organized challenge to the administration's use of authority, and so over the years they developed a sense of powerlessness in response to administrative decisions. The administration itself made few original decisions, but followed the dictates of the state department of education in developing curriculum and programs. At the bottom of the decision-making heap were the students, whose fate was tied up in their parents' uncertain job status. Students were granted little agency in determining the substance and process of their education. Students and faculty alike were far removed from authority and were strongly affected by the whims of distant forces in the economy, giving them the feeling of being pawns in a larger game played by invisible, powerful, indifferent hands.

Kathy Golden was one of the teachers in Pacific Hills who was "on the bubble." She was in her mid-forties, having married young and raised three children before returning to college to get her teaching credentials. Although she'd never been given a pink slip, she had little enough seniority that the threat of losing her job was everpresent. She had taught in Pacific Hills High School for five years now, one of ten English teachers for a school with a student body that fluctuated between 1,200 and 1,500, depending on the employment at the oil refinery. When she had started in the district there had been thirteen English teachers, but the faculty had been reduced through attrition and layoffs since, leaving her one good enrollment drop from unemployment.

Kathy taught freshmen and sophomores. For both preparations she was provided a curriculum that faithfully followed the literature anthology's organization. Learning objectives were handed down from the central curriculum office and were strictly based on the learner outcomes that were issued from the state department of education. Sophomores were scheduled to learn to write personal narratives and five-paragraph themes, know the parts of speech and the components of literary genres, and be knowledgeable in other such forms in order to pass the state-mandated assessment tests upon which each school's reputation was based. With real estate values tied to test scores, Pacific Hills's elected board of education placed a great deal of importance on these tests and evaluated administrators on the basis of test scores. Administrators, in turn, assessed each teacher's performance on the test scores of students.

The Pacific Hills schools, like schools throughout the country, participated in Red Ribbon Week, a national substance abuse awareness program in which schools devote attention across the curriculum to the dangers and prevention of drug and alcohol abuse. Ms. Golden had mixed feelings about Red Ribbon Week. On the one hand, she felt that it was important to raise health issues in school. She had known bright, potentially successful people who had developed drug or alcohol dependencies and ruined their personal relationships and professional opportunities. She felt that schools would be doing a disservice if they attended to students' cognitive needs and ignored their spiritual, emotional, and physical needs. While drugs and alcohol were threats to personal safety throughout the country, they seemed particularly ominous in Pacific Hills, where unemployment struck quickly and caused turmoil within families. Students had access to both alcohol and a variety of drugs, and used them both recreationally and to reduce the stress caused by the uncertainty in their lives. Drug and alcohol problems were a cause of truancy among students, and a concern among teachers for creating health and academic problems for students. Red Ribbon Week, then, served an important purpose in addressing a critical problem facing the community.

> [This book] assumes that programs are not the answers to the learning problems of students but that teachers are and that, indeed, good teachers create good programs, that the best programs are developed *in situ,* in response to the needs of individual student populations and as reflections of the particular histories and resources of individual [schools].
>
> Mina P. Shaughnessy, *Errors & Expectations,* p. 6.

Yet Red Ribbon Week troubled Ms. Golden for several different reasons. The program sought to create a special focus on drug and alcohol awareness and was typically implemented by stopping all customary teaching, shifting the focus to drugs and alcohol, and then returning to business as usual for the rest of the year. Ms. Golden felt that separating the issue out for its own special week raised only temporary awareness and then ignored this crucial problem for the rest of the year. Indeed, because the issue of substance abuse had its own exclusive week, many teachers did not devote additional attention to it.

The interruption of regular instruction for Red Ribbon Week always seemed to come at an inconvenient time. Ms. Golden was forced to jockey her teaching so that she brought something to conclusion at the right time, and she always seemed to give short shrift to some important aspect of instruction in order to make space for the program. Pedagogically, then, the program disrupted the rest of her instruction, causing her to regard it as just one more interruption in her effort to teach. The program, presented with no supportive context, was typically regarded by students as a "soft" week in their schedule when they attended assemblies, were presented with prepackaged materials, were told to "just say no" to drugs, and then returned to their normal schedules.

Her reservations about the program's lack of connection to the rest of the curriculum were exacerbated by what she felt was its emphasis on the substances themselves, not on the reasons that people use them. Based on her knowledge of adults who abused drugs and alcohol, Ms. Golden felt that telling students to "just say no" was insufficient in addressing substance abuse. In her view, people don't say no to *drugs;* people say no to *people.* She felt that an effective drug and alcohol abuse program, while emphasizing the medical evidence of the substances' destructiveness, also needed to examine the social conditions that lead to dependency.

> What seemed to be important on the part of school people was not a clear ideological position or a coherently constructed curriculum but simply keeping up with the times. While one may find isolated examples of a school curriculum that followed a consistent ideological line, for the most part, what emerged as the American curriculum in the twentieth century was a hodgepodge of contradictory reforms patched on to the conventional humanist curriculum.
>
> Herbert M. Kliebard, *Learning and Teaching the Ways of Knowing,* p. 7.

A firm believer in integrating instruction, after her first few years of participating in Red Ribbon Week activities with ambivalence, Ms. Golden began to look for ways to incorporate the program's substance abuse educational information into the curriculum without experiencing it as a disruption. In thinking about how to achieve this end, she developed several related goals: to embed the Red Ribbon Week activities into larger themes of the curriculum, to present substance abuse as a social problem rather than as a substance problem, and to develop instructional activities related to Red Ribbon Week emphases that simultaneously met curriculum objectives.

In looking over her sophomore literature anthology she saw some possibilities. The textbook was organized so that it could be taught either thematically or by genre. The literature was amenable to several themes, such as "Exploring Identity," "Values in Conflict," and "Courage" that addressed social issues implicated in drug and alcohol abuse. Ms. Golden decided that, rather than treating Red Ribbon Week activities as a disembodied unit of study, she would work them in thematically with the literature units she would teach in the regular curriculum. In so doing she could meet her goals of integrating the substance abuse program with students' efforts to construct meaning from literature and with their writing. Furthermore, Ms. Golden saw that by having students write personal narratives about their experiences with social pressures, she could help prepare them for the state writing assessment, which required them to produce a narrative under examination conditions.

[S]chools do not usually begin their analysis of students by asking what they can already do well. The emphasis, rather, is most often placed on what students do badly or not at all. The curriculum is then conceived as a process of filling in gaps to remediate deficiencies or exposing students to new material.

Richard W. Beach & James D. Marshall, *Teaching Literature in the Secondary School*, p. 124.

Ms. Golden wanted to establish a relationship among the Red Ribbon Week themes, the literary themes, and students' own life themes and experiences. The sophomore anthology's first theme, "Exploring Identity," included such works as Robert Frost's "The Road Not Taken," Nikki Giovanni's "Choices," Doris Lessing's "Through the Tunnel," and other selections that involved characters facing important choices, often in the face of pressures to act against their better judgment. Ms. Golden saw this unit as an excellent vehicle for helping students connect their literary study with their personal experiences and the themes of Red Ribbon Week.

She wanted the students to approach the issues by framing them in terms of their own experiences. The types of conflicts represented in the literature provided illustrations of the pressures that can lead to drug and alcohol abuse. If students could establish a prior framework based on the scripts of their personal experiences, then their subsequent consideration of literary characters—and ultimately their consideration of choices they would face with drugs and alcohol—would, she felt, be facilitated. She decided to have students develop the initial literary texts for the unit by writing about personal experiences they'd had with choices in the face of social pressure. They would thus be able to include their own personal stories along with the selections from the anthology as the literary material for the unit.

At the beginning of the first class of the unit, she gave students the following prompt: "Write about an experience you've had in which you were pressured to act in certain ways, and had to make a choice about which way to act. What were the circumstances? What were the choices? Who was pressuring you to do what? Why? What did you decide to do? Why? If put in the same situation again, what would you do this time?" Her purpose in giving this prompt was twofold: to have students develop a script for the literary conflicts they would later study, and to have students use writing as a way of exploring their ideas about the topic.

[W]riting can be a powerful process for discovering meaning rather than just transcribing an idea that is in some sense waiting fully developed in the writer's mind. Our language provides a whole panoply of devices that not only convey our meaning to others, but help us develop the meaning for ourselves. . . .

In our concern with writing as a way to express an idea or reveal subject-area knowledge, we tend to overlook the extent to which these devices help us generate new ideas "at the point of utterance."

Arthur N. Applebee, *Writing in the Secondary School,* p. 100.

One student, a girl named Lacey, produced the following narrative:

I was with my girlfriends before school one day and they started talking about how boring school was and how they didn't feel like going and about how they wanted to ditch school and go to the mall. Well I didnt want to but they started planning this whole thing like I was going with them and after they got it all planned I couldn't say no so I went with them. We werent doing anything in my classes so it didnt matter any if I missed so I figured I could miss one day and nobody would notice. We planned to call from the mall and disguise our voices and act like it was our parents calling about how sick we were so I figured no problem. Well we got to the mall and after a while we got bored their too so one of my girlfriends decided we needed to have a shoplifting contest to see who could rip off the most expensive thing. The winner would get to keep all the things that the others stole and the person who stoled the cheapest thing would have to call a real dorky guy on the phone and talk to him. Well I didnt want to shoplift or call up some dorky guy but I didnt have much choice so we decided to go to sears and split up and see who could steal the thing that cost the most, I have to confess I cheated, I went to the jewelry section and bought a pair of earrings for 15$ and pretended I riped it off. Lucky for me they didn't find out and also lucky for me someone else stole something cheaper. All in all I didn't mind giving the earrings to the girl that stole the most expensive thing which was some perfume but, unlucky for me the school called back my house to check about my sick call and my dad was home to let in a plummer in and I got caught ditching so I got grounded anyhow.

After they had produced these informal narratives, Ms. Golden asked the students to share them in small groups. She planned that these narratives would serve several purposes: (1) Form the basis for short plays that students would perform before the class. (2) Provide students with story scripts from their own experiences which in turn inform their understanding of the conflicts in the literature to be read, and provide the basis for their attention to the social pressures discussed during Red Ribbon Week activities that can lead to drug and alcohol abuse. (3) Serve as the initial consideration of a topic that students would later develop into a formal narrative to be turned in for a grade. (4) And finally, prepare students for the state writing assessment.

[In drama] movement and gesture play a larger part in the expression of meaning; a group working together upon an improvisation needs more deliberately and consciously to collaborate; the narrative framework allows for repetition and provides a unity that enables the action more easily to take on symbolic status—to have meaning beyond the immediate situation in which it occurs. . . . [Students can act out] in symbolic—and often unrealistic—form their fears, hatreds, and desires [to help] them assimilate those too disturbing to be acknowledged literally.

Douglas Barnes, *Drama in the English Classroom*, pp. 8–9.

The students used both the sharing day and the next day to develop their dramatic productions. Ms. Golden told them that they could either use one student's narrative as the basis for the play, or combine elements of several into a single story. In any case they were free to elaborate and fabricate to make the story more interesting and fun to produce. She recommended that they prepare and follow a script, although she did not insist on this feature for groups that performed better spontaneously. When they performed, students were encouraged to use props, music, special effects, or other resources to enhance their productions, although they were not allowed to use real drugs or alcohol in plays that focused on pressures to imbibe them.

Lacey got in a group with her friends Courtney, Jennifer, and Kay. After she read her narrative and talked about the adventure with her friends, Lacey heard the stories they'd written. Courtney had written about a time some friends had pressured her into going out to a quarry and diving off high rocks into a pool of water where a teenager had drowned a few years before after losing consciousness when he'd hit his head on the bottom after a dive. Jennifer had described an occasion when some friends had tried to get her to smoke cigarettes, even though her mother was quite ill with emphysema; she'd resisted the pressure but lost the friendships in the process. Kay had written about a time in math class when some friends had wanted to play a game of "chicken" where the winner was the one who called out the loudest profanity during class. Kay had lost the game but the winner had received several days of detention.

They discussed which play would make the best production. Kay's would require them to curse in class, which they got a chuckle out of, but which they thought would be inappropriate. Jennifer did not want to perform hers because she felt so strongly about her mother's declining health. Courtney's had potential, but they didn't know how they'd simulate the dives in the classroom. They therefore settled on Lacey's story, which they liked, which had a part for each of them, and which didn't require any special effects. They discussed ways they might embellish it: They could make Lacey lose and end up talking to the dorky guy, or they could have Lacey steal the earrings instead of buying them. After talking about the possibilities, they decided to leave Lacey's actions more or less the same, and improvise with the other three characters.

Students apply a wide range of strategies to comprehend, interpret, evaluate, and appreciate texts. They draw on their prior experience, their interactions with other readers and writers, their knowledge of word meaning and other texts, their word identification strategies, and their understanding of textual features (e.g., sound-letter correspondence, sentence structure, context, graphics).

They spent class time working out a script for the play. They decided to write out their lines and keep a script handy in case they forgot what to say or do, although they wanted to avoid reading the script during their performance. They figured that they didn't need special props; they could put four chairs together

and pretend it was a car for driving to the mall, they could simulate telephones by holding their hands to their ears, and they could use things they already had—earrings, perfume, a wallet, a hairbrush—to shoplift. To show that they felt that shoplifting was wrong, they decided to change the story so that Jennifer got caught stealing and was grounded for six months by her parents, and Courtney, who played the role of the girl who won the contest, ended up feeling guilty and mailing the contraband back to the store.

It took a class period to perform all the plays. One set of students performed a scene from a party where a boy was tempted by his friends to drink beer; he gave in to their pressure and drank several beers before getting sick and passing out on the lawn, where the police found him and returned him to his parents. Another group performed a play in which a student had been grounded and his friends persuaded him to sneak out through his window and join them for an evening of carousing, a night that ended with a car accident that brought in the police and resulted in an even longer grounding from his parents. Another play concerned a girl whose best friend wanted her to help cheat on a test by providing her with answers; the girl agreed to help but panicked during the test and didn't pass along the answers, causing her friend to shun her thereafter. The final play was about a girl who went out on Halloween with some friends who decided to blow up people's mailboxes with some big firecrackers they had left over from the Fourth of July; she went along with the group but successfully deflected efforts to get her to light the fuses until one of the boys in the group insisted that she light the fuse that they put in the mailbox of her parents' friends. She gave in to the pressure, lit the fuse, and exploded the mailbox, but felt terrible and confessed in church the following Sunday.

Following the production of the plays, Ms. Golden led a class discussion of the story featured in each drama. The class found remarkable consistency across the productions: Each one involved a character whose values were challenged when friends offered temptation and pressure to do something illicit. Although Ms. Golden was at times alarmed by the degree of temptation available to her students, she encouraged them to draw on their experiences to guide the discussion of the issues.

Ms. Golden then told the students that the literature they were going to read would be based on similar types of conflicts, although not necessarily featuring teenagers or the specific pressures they'd seen in the plays. She led the students through discussions of several works of literature from their anthology, including

Students read a wide range of literature from many periods in many genres to build an understanding of the many dimensions (e.g., philosophical, ethical, aesthetic) of human experience.

Daniel Inouye's "My Shirt Is for Church," Frost's "The Road Not Taken," and Giovanni's "Choices." With each selection she urged the students to consider the characters' dilemmas, the types of social forces conspiring to influence their choices, and the consequences of each decision they might make. Discussions were not confined to the text, but also included references to the student plays and other sources of student knowledge about social influences on personality development, including films, television programs, and episodes from their lives. When discussing "The Road Not Taken," for instance, Lacey referred back to her experience with ditching school and shoplifting, pointing out that while on one hand it was easier to go to school than to go out and shoplift, on the other hand it was easier to give in to peer pressure than to resist it and go to school. For her, the road less traveled was the road to resisting pressure, although it was a road she had difficulty taking.

Ms. Golden intended that the small-group plays and the whole-group discussions would scaffold the students' understanding of the story scripts found in much of the literature about personal choices within a social context, literature that found its basis in human experience. After helping to guide their initial explorations of these themes in teacher-led discussions, Ms. Golden asked students to work in small groups to examine unfamiliar stories involving a similar script. Students read Doris Lessing's "Through the Tunnel," a story about a young English boy vacationing with his widowed mother at a French villa. The boy, Jerry, meets some older, wilder, native boys who dive deep beneath the ocean's surface and swim through a subaquatic tunnel to prove their manhood. Jerry tries to dive with them but loses his nerve and surfaces as the older boys complete their dive. They then abandon him, leaving him feeling inadequate. He believes that he will not be considered a man unless he swims through the tunnel, and so spends his remaining vacation attempting dives; he finally succeeds on the last day, but nearly drowns in the process and is so exhausted that he feels no celebration or accomplishment from his achievement.

Ms. Golden provided the students with a heuristic to frame their discussion, based on both the story structure of their personal narratives and the questions they had posed when discussing literature in the teacher-led discussions:

What conflicts and choices does the character face in this story?

Who is pressuring the protagonist to do what? Why?

What did he decide to do? Why?

How do you evaluate this choice?

What is the basis of your evaluation?

If put in the same situation as the character was in, what would you do? Why?

Lacey got back into her group with Jennifer, Courtney, and Kay to discuss these questions. They began looking at the character and his response to the social pressure to dive through the tunnel and prove himself. Their discussion eventually turned to his maturity:

> *Courtney:* He had no self-confidence or he wouldn't need to dive through that tunnel.
>
> *Jennifer:* What do you think?
>
> *Courtney:* He's, um, shy. He was by himself. Kind of like being an outcast.
>
> *Lacey:* He was intimidated by those older guys because he was rich and sheltered, and they were so wild and could do things like dive through the tunnel.

Students read a wide range of print and nonprint texts to build an understanding of texts, of themselves, and of the cultures of the United States and the world; to acquire new information; to respond to the needs and demands of society and the workplace; and for personal fulfillment. Among these texts are fiction and nonfiction, classic and contemporary works.

Students use spoken, written, and visual language to accomplish their own purposes (e.g., for learning, enjoyment, persuasion, and the exchange of information).

Students apply knowledge of language structure, language conventions (e.g., spelling and punctuation), media techniques, figurative language, and genre to create, critique, and discuss print and nonprint texts.

Courtney: Yeah. Is he actually immature for these . . . I mean, how can you be immature?

Kay: It's, it's kind of like when you're not really mature until you're social. You can't be mature if you're some kind of hermit because then you'll never learn how to do the things that mature people do.

Lacey: Until you're social? Because you may be—so, a person's shy so they're—unsocial?

Kay: It takes a maturity to be social.

Lacey: No.

Kay: Yes, it does.

Lacey: No. Because his problem in the story was that he went through the tunnel because he was trying to be like those other guys, live up to somebody else's expectations. So he was being social, but I think that made him less mature because it made him take the road more traveled like what's-his-name the poet said, even though hardly anybody could make that dive, so it was less traveled and more traveled at the same time. I don't know. I'm kind of confused.

Jennifer: It's like that movie *Pretty in Pink* where the guy won't date the girl even though he really likes her because his high-class friends think she's geeky because of where she lives.

Lacey: Huh?

Jennifer: You know, it's easier to date her because he wants to, but it's also easier to put her down because that's what his friends expect, so it's harder and easier, but mostly harder no matter what he does.

Kay: But going through the tunnel made him more of a man, so he was more mature.

Courtney: Yeah.

Lacey: Yeah. But I mean, no, I don't believe you have to be social to mature, and I don't think you're a man just because you're macho.

Courtney: Ma-cho ma-cho ma-a-an.

Lacey: I think he gave in to the pressure just like I did when I ditched school. I was being social so, according to you, I was being mature, but I don't think so.

Courtney: But you are not as successful when you are, when you keep to yourself.

Lacey: So you have to be successful to be mature, too?

Courtney: Yes.

Lacey: Why? I mean, the kid in the story was successful because he finally swam through the tunnel, but he wasn't even happy about it, and he almost died anyhow.

Courtney: Well, the older guys probably still thought he was a dork because he was a rich kid. He might've swum through the tunnel, but they didn't accept him at the end of the story, so if he did it to get accepted, then it didn't even work.

Kay: Is "swum" a word?

Courtney: Who cares? I just used it, so it's a word. Anyhow, the boy in the story wanted to act like the older guys, so he risked his life. I think that's not mature even though it's social because he did it because of social pressure because he thought they ran away from him because he couldn't dive through the stupid tunnel. I think he just did it to be like everyone else, just like I did when I went diving at that quarry—I could have killed myself just like that other guy did and just like that kid in the story almost did.

Jennifer: So, that showed whatever-his-name-is's lack of immaturity, no, no, lack of maturity, um, that he wasn't independent enough to listen to himself. That he listened to others, no, he couldn't talk their language. He tried to be like them, which shows that even though he thought he was like the older guys he was actually doing something stupid.

The students continued to discuss the story in this fashion in response to the heuristic Ms. Golden had provided them. In their discussion they looked at the character in terms of their own narratives, the other literature they'd read, and other examples they generated about people in similar circumstances. Each group responded to these questions in writing and gave them to Ms. Golden. Ms. Golden didn't particularly like to require the written answers when students worked in small groups, but found that students were less likely to socialize off task if they produced a written response.

The students followed up their small-group discussions with a class discussion of the story in which they exchanged views developed in the small groups. As in Lacey's group, students disagreed over Jerry's obsession with going through the tunnel and his ultimate success in doing so: Did they represent a positive step forward or reveal his weakness in allowing social pressures to dictate his behavior? In exploring the question of whether the character had taken the road more or less traveled, students compared Jerry to their own narratives, to other people they knew, and to other characters from literature and popular culture. The issue remained unresolved; when the question came up about how the students would act if put in Jerry's situation, many views emerged concerning what would be the best course of action to take.

To see how well students had adopted these response procedures for their own purposes, the class read a play from their anthology, Reginald Rose's *Twelve Angry Men,* a drama in which one man resists pressure from eleven other jurors to quickly convict a boy accused of murder. The class read the play together, and then students used the questions from the heuristic that guided their small-group discussions to stimulate their response to the story. Lacey produced the following paper in response to the play:

12 Angry Men

This play is about a jury that's supposed to decide if a boy killed his father. Most of the jurors think the boy did it and just want to go home. One of them, #8, doesn't think so and tries to get the others to see if it's possible he's innocent. At the beginning of the play there's a description of all the jurors. Most of them are described with words like "Bitter" and "slick" and "dull-witted" but #8 is called "A quiet thoughtful man. A man who sees all sides of every question and constantly seeks the truth. A man of strength tempered with compassion. Above all, a man who wants justice to be done and will fight to see that it is." Well, after that introduction you know he's going to be right, and sure enough he is.

The other people on the jury though don't want to hear about it and are really mad that he tries to be fair. They complain about how long the trial took and about how hot it is. #7 wants to end their discussion quickly so he can go to a play. #10 thinks he's guilty because he's poor. #3 thinks that because he bought a knife he must be the killer. #8 is the only one who wants to talk about the possibility that he's innocent.

The other jurors all try to put pressure on #8 to convict the boy. When they count the votes #3 says "Somebody's in left field." When #8 asks if everyone thinks the boy lied #10 says "Now that's a stupid question." Other jurors almost try to fight him to get him to stop defending the boy. #3 even says he's going to kill him. But soon some of them start to come over to his side. #9 admires him because of his courage. Others do too and eventually they figure out that the boy was innocent.

Just as it said he would at the beginning, #8 stuck by his principles and didn't let the others pressure him into going along with their opinion. Because he cared about the truth and not about going to a play or something selfish he saved the boy's life. I hope that if I'm ever in a situation like that I'll do what's right and not let anybody else bully me into going along with their program. I admire people who stand up for what they believe in and hope that someday people will admire me for the way I act.

Students employ a wide range of strategies as they write and use different writing process elements appropriately to communicate with different audiences for a variety of purposes.

Following this writing, the students returned to their personal experience narratives that had formed the basis of their dramas. Ms. Golden both wanted to help students develop these into polished pieces of writing, and to help students develop strategies for producing narratives in response to prompts for the state writing assessment. The students would produce narratives for the state writing assessment during a controlled time period, and ultimately Ms. Golden felt that they needed some practice under time constraints. For their initial instruction, however, she wanted to regard writing as an extended process involving prewriting, drafting, revision, peer critiques, and other stages of writing that she knew many writers engage in when producing thoughtful manuscripts.

Students had already produced initial drafts and had read a variety of other texts that considered related issues. They therefore had been exposed to several literary narratives and poems that provided narrative elements for them. To identify these elements she decided to work inductively. From her files of student work from previous years, she selected a set of narratives representing a range of qualities that were often unevenly represented in single papers. One narrative, for instance, included a number of fascinating details and vivid images, yet had several spelling and grammar errors. Another provided a clear, linear account of an event, yet employed banal language and little sense of dramatic progression. Still another related the story well, yet was excessive and overly ornamental in its use of modifiers and similes. Ms. Golden took these essays and retyped them, excluding the original writers' names and manipulating them to provide contrasts in qualities.

She then asked students to form small groups and gave them a set of five essays, asking students to read them carefully and then rank them from best to worst. To produce this ranking each group needed to analyze their features and make value judgments on their relative qualities. Ms. Golden had prepared the narratives so that there was no clear hierarchy of quality; indeed, different groups came up with different rankings. The point of the activity was for students to use these essays to consider what they valued in narratives rather than for Ms. Golden to lead them toward a predetermined set of values.

Following the small-group work the students met as a class to discuss the sample narratives. Students discussed their relative rankings and why they had so judged them. Ms. Golden orchestrated the discussion, encouraging students to argue with one another over the merits of the papers. Through this discussion students identified a set of qualities that they felt should be included in effective narratives, such as a compelling and authentic story line, strong (but not overdone) images, a clear (although not necessarily linear) account of action, a portrayal of relationships, an absence of narrative explanation for events, and other features. Although their priorities differed for which features were most important, students generally agreed on those that needed to be present. Ms. Golden then informed the students that the criteria they had identified would be what she would ultimately use in grading their narratives.

Following this activity, Ms. Golden asked the students to produce a narrative related to the theme of exploring identity through choices in the face of social influence. They had the option of rewriting their original narratives or producing a new one. Students had one class period to produce drafts, plus whatever time they needed at home to complete them.

Lacey decided to revise her original story to try to make it more interesting. She got out her original narrative, read it, and then rewrote it as follows:

> My name is Lacey and I am a good girl. Or at least I try to be. One time my friends tried to get me to do things that I thought were wrong, because I was week I did them anyhow and lost the trust of my parents and my friendships also. I learned from this experience not to do things that other people want you to do, but just to do what's true to you. Here is my storry.
>
> I was with my girlfriends before school one day and they started talking about how boring school was and how they didn't feel like going, then they got this great idea to ditch school and go to the mall for the day. Well I sort of wanted to go and also didn't want to go. But they started planing this whole thing and before I knew it I was headed out to the mall in one of their cars. We werent doing anything in my classes so it didnt matter any if I missed so I figured I could miss one day and nobody would notice.
>
> Well we got to the mall and called school and disguised our voices and acted like it was our parents calling about how sick we were so I figured no problem. After we hung around for a while and had a coke and some donuts at the coffee shop we got bored so one of my girlfriends decided we needed to have a shoplifting contest to see who could rip off the most expensive thing. The winner would get to keep all the things that the others stole and the person who stoled the cheapest thing would have to call a real dorky guy on the phone and talk to him. Well I didn't want to shoplift or call up some dorky guy but I didn't have much choice so we decided to go to sears and split up and see who could steal the most expensive thing. I have to confess I cheated, I went to the jewelry section and bought a pair of earrings for 15$ and pretended I ripped it off. Lucky for me they didn't find out and also lucky for me someone else stole something cheaper, all in all I didn't mind giving the earrings to the girl that stole the most expensive thing which was some perfume. But unlucky for me the school called back my house to double check about my sick call and my dad just happened to be home. He'd come home from work to let a plummer in and answered the phone and it was the atendence office double checking my phone call. I got caut ditching so I got

Students apply knowledge of language structure, language conventions (e.g., spelling and punctuation), media techniques, figurative language, and genre to create, critique, and discuss print and nonprint texts.

grounded, I learned the hard way to do what you think is right, not what your friends want you to do. After that they weren't such good friends anyhow.

The students then brought their narratives to class and critiqued one another's papers in small groups. Each student used notes from class discussions as a critical guide in responding to their peers' narratives, and each student was responsible for noting the advice of other students to take into consideration for the revision. Students were required to turn in all drafts along with the final draft, including notes generated during peer revision.

Lacey's group provided her with some suggestions based on their ranking of the sample essays Ms. Golden had provided. Jennifer thought that she explained too much and needed to *show* the way she lost her friends, rather than coming right out and saying it. Kay said that the story would be more interesting if she included dialogue about their plans, rather than just saying that they decided to go to the mall and steal things. Courtney thought it was a good story, but that Lacey needed to work on her spelling and punctuation, and pointed out where Lacey could improve in these areas. After they had finished with Lacey's paper, they read each of the other students' narratives and critiqued them similarly.

Following the small-group responses, students took their narratives home for revision. Ms. Golden gave students several days to complete them and turn them in for a grade, using the criteria that the class had developed for assessment. Based on her group's advice, Lacey produced the following narrative:

The Day I Ditched

Caution: This is A TRUE STORY! The names have been changed to protect the guilty.

I was standing around before school when I saw some of my friends, Jackie, Allison, and Julie. We started talking.

"Another boring day at school" said Jackie.

"That's what you say everyday" I said.

"Well let's do something about it" said Julie. "Let's go out cruising at the mall."

"Yeah!" said Jackie. "Cruising at the mall!"

"I've got a car!" said Allison.

"Uh, I think I've got a math quiz" I said.

"No problemo!" said Julie. "We'll call in sick and you can make it up. Let's go!"

We got in the car and drove to the mall. When we got there Allison called the attendance office and said, "Hello I'm Jackie Davenport's mother and she has the flu, so she wont be coming to school today. Goodbye." A few minutes later Jackie called and said I was sick, then Jackie called and said Allison was sick, then finally I called and said Julie was sick. Then we went to the coffee shop and ate donuts for a while and drank Cokes.

Pretty soon we got bored with this. Allison said, "I know, let's go shopping."

Julie said, "Do you mean for those five finger discounts?"

"Of course!" Allison said. Then she said "I know let's make it interesting. Let's see who can rip off the most expensive thing."

"Yes!" said Jackie. "And whoever steals the most expensive thing, everybody else has to give her the stuff they stole."

I didn't like the sound of this, but then it got worse. "And who ever steals the cheapest thing has to call ... CHET PERKINS on the phone!"

Well we all laughed really hard at this since he's the dorkiest guy in the whole school. So then we got up and went to Sears for the shoplifting contest. We all went in separate directions so as not to make anyone suspicious. All the clerks seemed to be staring right at me so I was scared to steal anything. Finally I got a good idea, instead of stealing something Id buy something and pretend like I stole it. So I made sure noone was looking and bought a pair of ear rings for $15.

We met back at the coffee shop. Julie stole a bottle of perfume worth $25 and she won so we all gave her our stuff. Allison stole a hairbrush worth $10 and had to call Chet Perkins and talk to him.

We hung around until school was out and then went home. My dad was waiting there for me and boy was he mad. He'd come home from work to let a plumber in and answered the phone and it was the attendance office doublechecking my phone call. He grounded me for two months so that I had to come straight home from school every day and not ever go out with friends even on weekends. Even after I got ungrounded I didn't see those friends much any more.

In the months that followed the completion of their narratives, Ms. Golden periodically provided them with prompts for narratives that they would produce within time constraints. Following their writing she would have students critique one another's narratives and provide her own response as well, using the criteria they had developed during their ranking activity to evaluate the papers.

As Ms. Golden had planned, Red Ribbon Week occurred following the completion of the in-class attention to narratives. During Red Ribbon Week students were required to attend assemblies, listen to talks by recovering substance abusers, receive pamphlets and other information about substance abuse, and be spectators to other presentations related to the week's theme. A week before Red Ribbon Week, as students were working on their narratives, Ms. Golden assigned them to read *Alex the Great,* a young adolescent novel that presents a problematic friendship from the perspectives of its two main characters, Alex Starky and Deonna Johnson. The girls are best friends but their lives are going in different directions: Alex is routinely truant, takes and sells drugs, steals, and otherwise rebels against rules, while Deonna is a tennis star who follows a straighter path. Deonna must decide whether it's best for her friend to keep her out of trouble or turn her in. The book presents the themes of the literature they had been reading with a special focus on the ways in which social pressures can lead teenagers to get involved with addictive drugs, and the ways in which teenagers must consider what's best for their friends and their friendships.

During Red Ribbon Week, Ms. Golden's students read and talked about *Alex the Great* and about the influences and temptations that were available to them. Ms. Golden made an effort to weave "official" Red Ribbon Week materials into their discussions, providing specific information on particular drugs when their use came up, and inviting a school counselor to talk with students about how to resist the pressures brought on by other teenagers to experiment with drugs and alcohol. They discussed the particular issues of their community, such as the constant threat of unemployment that faced many of their families, and how to develop other resources for dealing with despair and loss. Students discussed behavior that followed from substance abuse, such as physical abuse, lack of responsibility, and lack of consideration for others. They further explored what to do in response to these behaviors and how to help friends who were allowing drugs and alcohol to affect their lives. In conjunction with information provided by Red Ribbon Week officials, students identified a great array of

Students read a wide range of literature from many periods in many genres to build an understanding of the many dimensions (e.g., philosophical, ethical, aesthetic) of human experience.

resources for avoiding the social pressure to engage in substance abuse, and for addressing problems of abuse when they developed among families and other social groups.

At the conclusion of Red Ribbon Week, Ms. Golden made certain to extend the lessons of the program into their continued explorations of literature. When studying other themes of the anthology, such as "Values in Conflict" and "Courage," students returned to the issues that were raised during their thematic unit on "Exploring Identity" and their connections to Red Ribbon Week. They continued to develop their ability to write narratives on themes related to the literature they studied, at times engaging in extended processes and at times producing them under exam conditions. Ms. Golden thus achieved her goal of integrating the program into the curriculum and tying student production to a personal exploration of important issues in their lives, to their informed reading of thematically related literature, and to their preparation for state-mandated writing assessments.

Standards in Practice

Students in Ms. Golden's class draw on a wide variety of sources to understand the ways in which social pressures can influence the directions their lives take. Ms. Golden asks them to consider their own experiences with peer pressure as a foundation for their reading and writing activities, and for their consideration of the Red Ribbon Week themes. These experiences then contribute to the development of students' own literary and dramatic texts that become part of the class's oeuvre of literary works, and that become key texts in their consideration of the moral issues involved in making personal decisions amidst social pressures. These personal texts further serve to inform their reading of literature that concerns social pressure, and of factual documents about substance abuse. Their consideration of their own experiences with peer influence is abetted by their involvement in extended writing. This attention to the process of writing enables them to consider carefully the elements that would contribute to an effective narrative, and also to consider at length their relationships with their peers through their continual attention to their personal experiences. Through their integration of their own experiences with different strands of the English language arts curriculum and the school substance abuse program, the students are encouraged to engage in literacy practices that help them reflect on, identify, and achieve their own goals.

Resources

Writing to Learn/Writing Across the Curriculum

Books and Articles

Ackerman, J. (1993). The promise of writing to learn, *Written Communication, 10*(3), 334–370.

Applebee, A. N. (1981). *Writing in the secondary school: English and the content areas.* NCTE Research Report No. 21. Urbana, IL: National Council of Teachers of English.

Atwell, N. (Ed.). (1990). *Coming to know: Writing to learn in the intermediate grades.* Portsmouth, NH: Heinemann.

Bazerman, C., & Russell, D. R. (Eds.). (1994). *Landmark essays on writing across the curriculum.* Davis, CA: Hermagoras Press.

Britton, J., Burgess, T., Martin, N., McLeod, A., & Rosen, H. (1975). *The development of writing abilities 11–18.* London: Macmillan Educational.

Elbow, P. (1973). *Writing without teachers.* New York: Oxford University Press.

Elbow, P. (1981). *Writing with power: Techniques for mastering the writing process.* New York: Oxford University Press.

Elbow, P. (1986). *Embracing contraries: Explorations in learning and teaching.* New York: Oxford University Press.

Emig, J. (1977). Writing as a mode of learning. *College Composition and Communication, 28*(2), 122–128.

Fulwiler, T., & Young, A. (Eds.). (1982). *Language connections: Writing and reading across the curriculum.* Urbana, IL: National Council of Teachers of English.

Gere, A. R. (Ed.). (1985). *Roots in the sawdust: Writing to learn across the disciplines.* Urbana, IL: National Council of Teachers of English.

Langer, J. A., & Applebee, A. N. (1987). *How writing shapes thinking: A study of teaching and learning.* NCTE Research Report No. 22. Urbana, IL: National Council of Teachers of English.

Mayher, J. S., Lester, N. B., & Pradl, G. M. (1983). *Learning to write/writing to learn.* Upper Montclair, NJ: Boynton/Cook Publishers.

Moffett, J. (1981). *Active voice: A writing program across the curriculum.* Upper Montclair, NJ: Boynton/Cook Publishers.

Murray, D. M. (1984). *Write to learn.* New York: Holt, Rinehart, and Winston.

Tchudi, S., & Yates, J. (1983). *Teaching writing in the content areas: Senior high school.* Washington, D.C.: NEA Professional Library.

E-mail Network

wac-l@uiucvmd.bitnet

Using Drama in the Classroom

Books and Articles

Barnes, D. (1968). *Drama in the English classroom: Papers relating to the Anglo-American seminar on the teaching of English at Dartmouth College, New Hampshire, 1966.* Champaign, IL: National Council of Teachers of English.

Bolton, G. M. (1984). *Drama as education: An argument for placing drama at the centre of the curriculum.* Harlow, Essex, England: Longman.

Booth, D. (1987). *Drama words.* Toronto: Language Study Centre.

Byron, K. (1986). *Drama in the English classroom.* New York: Methuen.

Christen, L. (1993). *Drama skills for life: A handbook for secondary teachers.* Portsmouth, NH: Heinemann.

Felton, M., Little, G., Parsons, B., & Schaffner, M. (1984). *Drama, language, and learning.* (NADIE Paper, No. 1). Australia: National Association for Drama in Education.

Johnson, L., & O'Neill, C. (Eds.). (1984). *Dorothy Heathcoate: Collected writings on education and drama.* London: Hutchinson.

King, N. (1993). *Storymaking and drama: An approach to teaching language and literature at the secondary and post-secondary levels.* Portsmouth, NH: Heinemann.

O'Neill, C., & Lambert, A. (1982). *Drama structures: A practical handbook for teachers.* London: Hutchinson.

O'Neill, C., Lambert, A., Linnell, R., & Warr-Wood, J. (1977). *Drama guidelines.* London: Heinemann.

Pavis, P. (1982). *Languages of the stage: Essays in the semiology of the theatre.* New York: Performing Arts Journal Publications.

Smagorinsky, P., & Coppock, J. (1995). Reading through the lines: An exploration of drama as a response to literature. *Reading & Writing Quarterly: Overcoming learning disabilities, 11*(4), 369–391.

Wagner, B. J. (Ed.). (in press). *What is learned through classroom drama.* Portsmouth, NH: Heinemann.

Instructional Scaffolding

Books and Articles

Applebee, A., & Langer, J. (1983). Instructional scaffolding: Reading and writing as natural language activities. *Language Arts, 60*(2), 168–175.

Dyson, A. H. (1990). Weaving possibilities: Rethinking metaphors for early literacy development. *The Reading Teacher, 44*(3), 202–213.

Flower, L. (1981). *Problem-solving strategies for writing.* New York: Harcourt Brace Jovanovich.

Hillocks, G., Jr. (1975). *Observing and writing.* Urbana, IL: ERIC Clearinghouse on Reading and Communication Skills and National Council of Teachers of English.

Hillocks, G., Jr. (1986). *Research on written composition: New directions for teaching.* Urbana, IL: ERIC Clearinghouse on Reading and Communication Skills and National Conference on Research in English.

Hillocks, G., Jr. (1995). *Teaching writing as reflective practice.* New York: Teachers College Press.

Johannessen, L., Kahn, E., & Walter, C. (1982). *Designing and sequencing prewriting activities.* Urbana, IL: ERIC Clearinghouse on Reading and Communication Skills and National Council of Teachers of English.

Kahn, E., Walter, C., & Johannessen, L. (1984). *Writing about literature.* Urbana, IL: ERIC Clearinghouse on Reading and Communication Skills and National Council of Teachers of English.

Lindemann, E. (1982). *A rhetoric for writing teachers.* New York: Oxford University Press.

Smagorinsky, P., & Gevinson, S. (1989). *Fostering the reader's response: Rethinking the literature curriculum, grades 7–12.* Palo Alto, CA: D. Seymour Publications.

Smith, M., & Hillocks, G., Jr. (1988). Sensible sequencing: Developing knowledge about literature text by text. *English Journal, 77*(6), 44–49.

Zemelman, S., & Daniels, H. (1988). *A community of writers: Teaching writing in the junior and senior high school.* Portsmouth, NH: Heinemann.

Teaching Writing as a Process

Books, Chapters, and Articles

Applebee, A. (1986). Problems in process approaches: Toward a reconceptualization of process instruction. In A. R. Petrosky & D. Bartholomae (Eds.), *The teaching of writing: The eighty-fifth yearbook of the National Society for the Study of Education, part 2* (pp. 95–113). Chicago: The University of Chicago Press and the National Society for the Study of Education.

Berthoff, A. (1978). *Forming, thinking, writing.* Rochelle Park, NJ: Hayden Book Co.

Emig, J. (1971). *The composing processes of twelfth graders.* NCTE Research Report No. 13. Urbana, IL: National Council of Teachers of English.

Emig, J. (1983). *The web of meaning: Essays on writing, teaching, learning, and thinking.* D. Goswami & M. Butler (Eds.). Upper Montclair, NJ: Boynton/Cook Publishers.

Hillocks, G., Jr. (1975). *Observing and writing.* Urbana, IL: ERIC Clearinghouse on Reading and Communication Skills and National Council of Teachers of English.

Hillocks, G., Jr. (1986). The writer's knowledge: Theory, research, and implications for practice. In A. R. Petrosky & D. Bartholomae (Eds.), *The teaching of writing: The eighty-fifth yearbook of the National Society for the Study of Education, part 2* (pp. 71–94). Chicago: The University of Chicago Press and the National Society for the Study of Education.

Hillocks, G., Jr. (1995). *Teaching writing as reflective practice.* New York: Teachers College Press.

Johannessen, L., Kahn, E., & Walter, C. (1982). *Designing and sequencing prewriting activities.* Urbana, IL: ERIC Clearinghouse on Reading and Communication Skills and National Council of Teachers of English.

Kahn, E., Walter, C., & Johannessen, L. (1984). *Writing about literature.* Urbana, IL: ERIC Clearinghouse on Reading and Communication Skills and National Council of Teachers of English.

Kirby, D., Liner, T., & Vinz, R. (1988). *Inside out: Developmental strategies for teaching writing.* Portsmouth, NH: Boynton/Cook Publishers.

Lindemann, E. (1982). *A rhetoric for writing teachers.* New York: Oxford University Press.

Macrorie, K. (1970). *Telling writing.* New York: Hayden Book Co.

Moffett, J. (1988). *Coming on center: Essays in English education.* Portsmouth, NH: Boynton/Cook Publishers.

Moffett, J., & Wagner, B. J. (1992). *A student-centered language arts curriculum, grades 7–12* (4th ed.). Portsmouth, NH: Heinemann.

Murray, D. M. (1968). *A writer teaches writing: A practical method of teaching composition.* Boston: Houghton Mifflin.

Murray, D. M. (1991). *The craft of revision.* Fort Worth: Holt, Rinehart, and Winston.

Newkirk, T. (1986). *To compose: Teaching writing in the high school.* Portsmouth, NH: Heinemann.

Newkirk, T. (Ed.). (1990). *To compose: Teaching writing in high school and college.* Portsmouth, NH: Heinemann.

Perl, S., & Wilson, N. (1986). *Through teachers' eyes: Portraits of writing teachers at work*. Portsmouth, NH: Heinemann.

Power, B. M., & Hubbard, R. (1991). *Literacy in process: Resource guide for teachers*. Portsmouth, NH: Heinemann.

Proett, J., & Gill, K. (1986). *The writing process in action: A handbook for teachers*. Urbana, IL: National Council of Teachers of English.

Rief, L. (1992). *Seeking diversity: Language arts with adolescents*. Portsmouth, NH: Heinemann.

Romano, T. (1987). *Clearing the way: Working with teenage writers*. Portsmouth, NH: Heinemann.

Tobin, L., & Newkirk, T. (Eds.). (1994). *Taking stock: The writing process movement of the 90s*. Portsmouth, NH: Boynton/Cook Publishers.

Zemelman, S., & Daniels, H. (1988). *A community of writers: Teaching writing in the junior and senior high school*. Portsmouth, NH: Heinemann.

Journals

College Composition and Communication, National Council of Teachers of English

Composition Chronicle: A Newsletter for Writing Teachers, Viceroy Publications

English Journal, National Council of Teachers of English

Exercise Exchange: A Journal of English in High Schools and Colleges, Clarion (PA) University

Focuses, Appalachian State (NC) University

Issues in Writing, Department of English, University of Wisconsin–Stevens Point

Journal of Advanced Composition, Association of Teachers of Advanced Composition

Journal of Basic Writing, City University of New York

Journal of Teaching Writing, Indiana Teachers of Writing

Quarterly, Center for the Study of Writing, University of California–Berkeley

Reading & Writing Quarterly, Hemisphere Publishing Corporation

Research in the Teaching of English, National Council of Teachers of English

Rhetoric Review, Rhetoric Review Association of America

Teachers and Writers Magazine, Teachers and Writers Collaborative

Teaching English in the Two-Year College, National Council of Teachers of English

The Writing Center Journal, National Writing Centers Association

The Writing Instructor, English Department, University of Southern California

Writing Lab Newsletter, National Writing Centers Association: An NCTE Assembly

Writing on the Edge, Campus Writing Center, University of California–Davis

Written Communication, Sage Publications

Organizations and Committees

National Writing Centers Association: An NCTE Assembly

NCTE Commission on Composition

NCTE Committee on Teaching the Conventions of Writing within the Context of the Student's Own Writing

NCTE Conference on College Composition and Communication

Penn State Conference on Rhetoric and Composition

E-mail Networks

These networks serve members of the Conference on College Composition and Communication, NCTE's college writing section.

pretext@miavx1.bitnet

ptissues@miamiu.acs.muohio.edu

purtopoi@purccvm.bitnet

rhetntl@mizzou1.missouri.edu

wcenter@unicorn.acs.ttu.edu

wpa-l@asuacad.bitnet

Young Adult Literature Concerning Substance Abuse

Novels, Biographies, and Autobiographies

Brooks, B. (1989). *No kidding.* Cambridge: Harper & Row.

Cole, B. S. (1989). *Alex the great.* New York: Rosen Publishing Group.

Cole, L. (1989). *Never too young to die: The death of Len Bias.* New York: Pantheon.

Irwin, H. (1990). *Can't hear you listening.* New York: Margaret K. McElderry Books.

Miklowitz, G. D. (1989). *Anything to win.* New York: Delacorte Press.

Morrison, M. A. (1989). *White rabbit: A doctor's story of her addiction and recovery.* New York: Crown.

Riddell, R. (1989). *Shadow witch.* New York: Atheneum.

Thompson, T. (1973). *Richie: The ultimate tragedy between one decent man and the son he loved.* New York: Saturday Review Press.

CHAPTER TWO

PERSPECTIVES ON *HUCKLEBERRY FINN*

Joe Gorin taught English and speech at Lafayette Heights High School, a large (3,500 students) suburban high school outside a Northeastern city. The school's setting gave it a highly diverse student body. On one border of the town was Jefferson, a semi-urban, primarily minority community whose residents worked a variety of jobs in the vicinity, often for hourly wages with no health or retirement benefits. A second neighboring town, Iron City, consisted primarily of white, ethnic, blue-collar families whose breadwinners were employed in trades, factories, and other occupations not requiring a college education. For both of these neighboring communities, a move to Lafayette Heights was considered a great sign of upward mobility; these towns were the primary sources of new residents to Lafayette Heights, with the school system often cited as a chief reason for relocation. New residents from these communities typically moved to one of the many rental units on the town's east side or bought modest homes south of the interstate highway that cuts across the lower third of town.

The north side of Lafayette Heights, where the high school was located, was more affluent than either the east or south sides. It was the home of many white-collar professionals, including doctors, business executives, lawyers, and others who could afford the large homes resting on spacious lots of wooded property. Of the lower-income residents who lived in the rental units on the east side, most tended to be minorities, primarily African Americans. The south-side neighborhoods below the interstate highway, known collectively as "Little Iron City," were mainly occupied by white, ethnic, working-class families.

The high school's diversity, while making it a vital place to teach and learn, also caused it to balance unsteadily on a mixture of racial, ethnic, and socioeconomic tensions. Residents of Jefferson and Iron City were notoriously at odds with one another and brought their antagonisms with them when they moved to Lafayette Heights. Students from different socioeconomic backgrounds often developed resentments that emerged in the school hallways and classrooms. School administrators had reluctantly developed a security force to patrol the school and its grounds to keep student hostilities at bay and to keep out non-students who entered school property to sell drugs, entice students out of classes, and otherwise disrupt the educational process. While there were no metal detectors at the doors, students were required to carry photo IDs and an underlying uneasiness to human relations permeated the school.

These tensions reflected larger social relationships in the community. Many African American parents, convinced that the school institution was racist, formed an association that aggressively challenged the school's policies, pointing to inequitable suspension rates for black and white students, disproportionate numbers of black students in basic track classes, unrepresentative numbers of minority faculty, a lack of African American perspectives throughout the curriculum, and other indicators of systemic racial inequality. The high school did have an African American assistant principal in charge of discipline, a former marine with rigid views on behavior who administered suspensions to students. However, although he was highly regarded by most faculty members, he was often viewed by African American parents as a pawn of the predominantly white board of education.

Even among the African American advocacy group there was dissension. Power struggles broke out and eventually two sets of parents quit the association to form their own groups, one more radical than the original and one more moderate. White parents, while less officially organized, were similarly active in presenting their interests to the teachers, administration, and board of education, often positioning themselves against the minority parents in their efforts to influence the direction of the school system. With such contention, few residents were happy with the quality of the educational process, even though families from neighboring communities continued to move to Lafayette Heights to take advantage of its superior schools. The ambivalence toward the school system was reflected in the citizenry's support of bond issues to fund education: they either passed by the slimmest of margins or were defeated.

In the midst of this often vituperative discord toiled a well-educated, highly professional faculty. Their efforts seemed more frustrating with each passing year as tensions within the community mounted. And their frustration often caused strife within the ranks. Some teachers believed it was important to understand equity issues raised by African American parents and devoted energy to making the school more representative of the community's changing demographics in its content and process. Others felt that any changes the school made in the interest of diversity inherently lowered the quality of education and kowtowed to special interests within the community at the expense of the school's longstanding reputation for academic achievement. The faculty were not divided on these issues by race, as was much of the community; both African American and white teachers defended the school's traditional values, and members of both races also questioned them. These conflicting orientations further complicated life in a school already pushed to the limits of its ability to function cohesively.

Administrators tried to address the turmoil through a number of different inservice programs, most of which created more dissatisfaction than they dissipated. One, devoted to "learning styles," raised questions about whether people of different races and cultural groups have different learning styles. This debate became angry when faculty who believed strongly in the established curriculum felt that accommodating a panoply of learners would "water down" the curriculum and undermine the school's reputation for academic excellence, a reputation that rested on the very values that were being questioned in the learning styles debate. Their reaction created additional anger on the part of those faculty who believed it was necessary to take students' cultural backgrounds into consideration when addressing their behavior and academic performance. A similar reaction followed an inservice presentation on black vernacular English, with some faculty adamant about the need for students to acquire standard diction to compete in the economy, and others similarly resolute about students' rights to their own language. These debates among the faculty paralleled the controversy that permeated relations throughout the community.

Joe Gorin, like a number of his colleagues, found that the tensions of the community affected his teaching. Some of the tensions were positive; in spite of how unsettling the discussions surrounding the inservices were, they forced him to reexamine his teaching in light of cultural issues. Others were less productive, such as the more open hostilities that were developing among some students and teachers. At times these hostilities were unrelated to the course content; some students simply didn't like each other or were playing out conflicts that had begun elsewhere. At other times, however, the conflicts that developed in Mr. Gorin's class were a consequence of his students' engagement with literature and the issues raised, intentionally or otherwise, by the authors.

Such a situation occurred with the junior year American literature curriculum. The curriculum followed the traditional chronological approach to American literature, covering the established canon of literary works. As a result, the students' only exposure to African American society in the entire first semester was through a brief excerpt from the slave narratives of Frederick Douglass; in the second semester the most prominent African American character was Jim, the runaway slave in *The Adventures of Huckleberry Finn*. With the African American advocacy groups in the community continually criticizing Lafayette Heights High School for its exclusion of an African American perspective in both the curriculum and in the development of school policy, Mr. Gorin became increasingly troubled about the limited presence of African American voices in the literature curriculum, and about the ways in which the only other portrayal of blacks—through Huck's racist narration in *Huckleberry Finn*—affected both his African American and white students.

Huckleberry Finn had always been a favorite novel of Joe Gorin's. He had read and studied it in high school, college, and as a graduate student, and always found something new in its insights about society. Jim was among his favorite literary characters because of his great resilience and dignity in the face of Huck's racism. Because he had never been called "nigger" himself, Mr. Gorin could read the language of the novel and distance himself from the abusive term. Over the years his African American students had complained about having to read a novel where the term "nigger" was used so frequently, but Mr. Gorin was convinced that they needed to get beyond their hurt feelings and take a more detached academic approach to the novel. *Huck Finn* was clearly a masterpiece of American letters, thought Mr. Gorin, and Twain's use of the word "nigger" was ironic. For many years he told his black students that they needed to transcend their initial emotional response to the term and achieve the proper distance to see Twain's larger purpose. That most African American students failed to do so, Mr. Gorin attributed to their lack of maturity as both students and individuals.

[I]f the school has one main goal, a goal that guides the establishment and priority of all others, it should be to promote the growth of students as healthy, competent, moral people. This is a huge task to which all others are properly subordinated.

Nell Noddings, *The Challenge to Care in Schools*, p. 10.

Yet as community tensions grew and Mr. Gorin increasingly listened to the varied perspectives being voiced on racial issues, his apprehension grew over his students' response to Huck's racism. As he listened to his African American students' pain in reading the novel, he began to question his hierarchy, one that viewed emotional response as less important and less intellectual than the conventional detached analysis. Mr. Gorin's instructional approach to the novel had always been for him to lead student discussions of the novel, and through this arrangement he had always suppressed any complaints about the novel's emotional impact on readers by telling students that they needed to move beyond their initial affective response and take the more appropriate analytic stance that would enable them to see the novel's ironic intention and great literary merit. Students who remained, in Mr. Gorin's view, stuck at the emotional level could never become advanced readers of the sort envisioned by the school's curriculum objectives and prized by colleges, the optimal destination for students implied in the high school's mission statement.

In typical classrooms, the most important asymmetry in the rights and obligations of teacher and students is over control of the right to speak. To describe the difference in the bluntest terms, teachers have the right to speak at any time and to any person; they can fill any silence or interrupt any speaker; they can speak to a student anywhere in the room and in any volume or tone of voice. And no one has the right to object. But not all teachers assume such rights or live by such rules all the time.

Courtney Cazden, *Classroom Discourse*, p. 54.

This attitude was quite different from the view he held in the speech classes he taught, where emotional and dramatic interpretation of texts was essential. As he considered the paradox of his conflicting values, he thought about conversations with his adult friends about their own reading, which revealed that they often had purely emotional responses to their experiences with literature, and indeed rarely engaged in the sort of intellectual analysis usually prized in English classes. Mr. Gorin began to wonder about the quality of affective experiences with literature and their place in the classroom. For mature, intelligent adults, *crying* was an appropriate response to powerful literature; yet tears were considered trivial in the classroom. With this thought in mind, Mr. Gorin began to reconsider how he might teach *Huckleberry Finn* in a way that allowed students affective response, that provided students a greater role in constructing a meaning for the novel, and that granted students greater authority in determining the processes of classroom discussion.

To accomplish these goals Mr. Gorin needed to change the organization of his classroom so that he wasn't solely responsible for setting the agenda for discussions. Typically, he engaged his students in what he referred to as Socratic dialogues in which he primarily served to ask students questions and then respond to their answers. Upon reflection, he realized that his students rarely posed their own questions; rather, they assumed that all discussion would issue from his own decisions about what was important in the literature. As a student, his own greatest successes had come from his efforts to pose his own questions, and he decided that he would like his students to develop the same capacity. As an experiment he asked students to pose their own questions in response to a reading assignment. To his dismay, the questions they developed all resembled the sort of factual questions often found at the end of selections in literature anthologies. With this realization he decided that *teaching students to ask questions* would be among the primary goals of his next effort to teach *Huckleberry Finn.*

There are some very good reasons why students do not ask questions, and these reasons are also very big ones—the predominant goals of education, the structures of the school, the relations between adults and children, the socialization into institutional and situational authority roles. As student questioning has been inhibited—in greater part—by these systemic conditions since the onset of observational research around the turn of the century, and as no contemporary factors can be perceived that might cause such change, no enhancement of student questioning in our lifetime will be observed. Schooling will be a process of knowledge transmission, and learning will not become a process of knowledge seeking.

J. T. Dillon, "The Remedial Status of Student Questioning," pp. 207–208.

Mr. Gorin decided that students needed to know how to pose different types of questions. For one set of questions, he relied on cognitive taxonomies to identify a set of queries requiring increasing levels of inference. These taxonomies would help students pose the type of question he customarily asked when he led them in discussions of literature. To achieve his goal of promoting affective response to literature, he also tried to think of question types that

would encourage students to explore their emotional response to literature. Finally, he decided to provide students with some ideas on how to get discussion participants to elaborate on their remarks. Teaching students how to pose all three types of questions, he felt, would enable them to construct meanings for the story that were not so heavily influenced by his own priorities of interpretation.

Mr. Gorin thus came up with the following plan: He would devote several days of class time to teaching students how to ask different kinds of questions, and have them practice developing questions on a short story they would read together. When he was satisfied that students could pose stimulating questions, he would ask groups of students to be responsible for different segments of *Huckleberry Finn,* have them develop questions on their sections, and then have each group lead the class in discussion for one period over the portion of the novel they'd chosen. His own role during these discussions would be to evaluate the discussion leaders' performance.

Before beginning his formal instruction in how to generate questions, Mr. Gorin told students to begin reading the novel, giving them three weeks outside class to complete it before their discussion-leading responsibilities began. Their outside reading came during a time when they spent class time preparing for, and then taking, state-mandated standardized tests. Following the testing period he devoted class time to teaching students how to generate particular types of questions. The questions were of the three types he had previously identified: "cognitive" questions that promoted the analytic response to literature that he had learned in college and that were customary throughout his English department; "affective" questions that solicited attitudes and feelings in response to the literature; and questions that prompted students to elaborate on their thoughts.

From the cognitive taxonomies he consulted, Mr. Gorin developed seven types of "cognitive" questions:

Textually Explicit Questions
1. *Basic stated information:* Asks for a key fact that is fundamental to grasping the essential action and/or relationships of the story.
2. *Key detail:* Asks for a detail that is key to the development of the plot.
3. *Stated relationship:* Asks for a directly stated relationship (often causal) between at least two pieces of information in the story.

Textually Implicit Questions
4. *Simple implied relationship:* Asks for a relationship that is not directly stated in the text.
5. *Complex implied relationship:* Asks about relationships that must be inferred from many different pieces of information.

Scriptally Implicit Questions
6. *Author's generalization:* Asks for an inference on what the whole literary text implies about the human condition.
7. *Structural generalization:* Asks how parts of the work operate together to achieve certain effects.

Mr. Gorin then began to consider the issue of developing affective questions. To do so he needed to look outside his school experiences and professional training, all of which informed his understanding of the academic approaches to literature, but few of which were helpful in fostering an emotional response to it. He thought of his own personal reading, his discussions of books and movies with friends, and his knowledge from reading feminist critiques of schooling. He came up with a set of questions that he hoped might encourage students to talk about how the literature made them feel:

1. *Emotional response:* Asks about the types of emotions readers feel in response to the literature, and the source of those emotions (both textual and personal).
2. *Affect:* Asks about the extent to which readers do and do not like the literature, and points to sources for that response (both textual and personal).
3. *Connections:* Asks about the degree to which readers relate to the characters and situations of the literature.

4. *Future action:* Asks readers how their reading of the literature will affect their own future action.

5. *Context:* Asks readers to reflect on the context of their reading (cultural background, social circumstances) and consider how that context has affected their response to the story.

By teaching students to pose such questions, Mr. Gorin hoped to enable a personal response to literature, a response that his students could reconsider in light of the contributions that others made to the discussions.

The final type of question developed by Mr. Gorin was an elaboration prompt, a simple device that requested a speaker to say more. It could come in two forms:

1. *General:* General prompts would take the same form regardless of the content of a student's remark. It might consist of a simple "Yes?" or request further explanation: "Could you elaborate on that?" or "What do you mean by that?"

2. *Specific:* Specific remarks build on something specific a student has said, and requests elaboration. It might consist of the repetition of a student's remark as an interrogative ("Huck is ignorant?"), or take a phrase from a student's remark and request elaboration about it ("Why do you think Jim should have abandoned Huck?").

To teach his students how to pose questions, Mr. Gorin decided to scaffold their learning by beginning with teacher-led, whole-class instruction, and then by having students work together in small groups to develop their own questions based on the question types he taught them. After evaluting these questions, the students would take responsibility for a certain set of chapters from *Huckleberry Finn* and then lead the class in a discussion over those chapters.

[T]hus, the reader must be active and responsible. He cannot be simply receptive, waiting to be provided with interpretations, to have significances pointed out and implications developed for him. To do so is to accept someone else's reading uncritically, adopting another's feelings and thoughts as one's own. Encouraging that docility makes for placid, malleable, lazy students, and places the English teacher in an untenable position, diminishing his role from that of teacher to that of spiritual leader, charged with the unethical task of molding his students.

Robert E. Probst, *Response and Analysis*, p. 24.

Mr. Gorin wanted to accomplish two goals at once. The first goal was to teach students how to generate questions. The second was to introduce students to the themes of *Huckleberry Finn* by having them read a thematically-related short story that would prepare them for Twain's satirical look at a hypocritical society. He selected the short story "Harrison Bergeron" by Kurt Vonnegut for this introductory purpose because of its accessibility and because it paralleled the genre and themes of *Huckleberry Finn*. The satirical story is set in the future when a hypocritical totalitarian government handicaps any citizen who has any advantage over any other. George and Hazel Bergeron's son Harrison is a highly intelligent, athletic young man who carries extensive handicaps, and who rebels against the government by casting off his handicaps, only to be shot down by Diana Moon Glampers, a highly placed government official.

Students began by reading the story silently. When they were finished, Mr. Gorin passed out a sheet that defined the seven types of cognitive questions he had developed and told them of his plan to teach them how to ask questions so they could lead their own discussions. "What are *you* going to do?" asked Gayle.

"I'm going to sit in the back of the room and listen to you talk," he replied. "Each group will get a grade on how well their questions stimulate a discussion. The more people who participate in the discussion, the better off you'll be. If you want people to participate in the discussions that *you* lead, then I recommend that you help them out by contributing to the discussions *they* lead."

For the initial instruction in how to generate questions, Mr. Gorin led the whole class together, starting by modeling how to ask each question type. He began with the simplest question, *basic stated information.* After reviewing the definition from the handout, he provided an example for "Harrison Bergeron": "How intelligent are George and Hazel?" He followed this by asking students to develop their own basic-stated-information questions for the story.

"How about, 'What's the title of the story?'" asked Jack.

"Well, what do you think?" Joe Gorin responded, gazing out at the class.

"Well, you don't need to read the story to be able to answer it, so I don't think so," said Mariam.

"Have you got a better question?" asked Mr. Gorin.

Mariam thought. "How about, 'What is George wearing?' You have to read the story to know that, plus if you don't know about the handicaps, then you're never going to understand the story."

"Sounds good," said Mr. Gorin. "Let's try one more." After the students generated another question, Mr. Gorin repeated the process with the second, and continued in this fashion until the class was presented with, and subsequently generated, questions of each type, with responses discussed for each. The illustrations Mr. Gorin gave for the remaining question types were:

Key detail: What is the purpose of each of George's handicaps?

Stated relationship: What does George think of the handicapping system established by the government? Where in the story do you find his views stated?

Simple implied relationship: Why does the description of Harrison spoken by the ballerina on television indicate that he is "extremely dangerous" to the government?

Complex implied relationship: What does George and Hazel's reaction to Diana Moon Glampers's ultimate action against Harrison tell you about the government's influence on their thinking?

Author's generalization: Compare the situation in this story to one in the real world. Your analogy need not involve government, but may concern any authority structure. What is the author trying to tell readers about human society?

Structural generalization: In what ways do George and Hazel change from the beginning of the story to the end? What is the author saying about the human condition based on the development of these characters?

Mr. Gorin next handed out a sheet that included definitions for each of the affective question types he had developed, and went through the same process with each one: defining the question type, illustrating it with an example from "Harrison Bergeron," and then having students develop similar questions. He started with *questions about emotional response* that ask about the types of emotions readers feel in response to the literature, and the source of those emotions (both textual and personal). To illustrate this type of question for "Harrison Bergeron," he asked, "Describe the emotions you felt as you read the story. Why do you feel this way?" He then asked students if they could think of similar questions.

Noah raised his hand and said, "Some people might not really get emotional about this story. So I'd ask, 'Did you have any emotions about what happened in the story?' For me, the answer would be no, unless you count laughing at the funny parts as being emotional."

The class agreed with Noah that not all stories prompt strong emotions in readers. Mr. Gorin cautioned students to avoid posing questions with yes/no answers, so Noah rephrased the question as, "What, if any, emotions did you have as you read the story?" Mr. Gorin then went on to the next question. He again repeated the process for each question type and provided the following examples for the remaining question types:

Questions about affect: What parts of the story did you like or dislike?

Questions about connections: Have you ever been in a situation when you felt the same way as any of the characters in the story?

Questions about future action: What has this story taught you about how to act in situations of this kind?

Questions about context: Are there any events from your personal life or from current events that have affected the way you feel about this story?

Finally, Mr. Gorin provided students with ideas on how to get other students to elaborate on their responses, introducing them to both general and specific prompts. To illustrate how to use them, he posed one of the questions from the examples he'd given to the class for discussion. "What has this story taught you about how to act in situations of this kind?"

"Well," said Savannah, "I sure wouldn't act like Hazel. I'd rather rebel the way Harrison did than be a bump on a log like Hazel."

"Please go on," said Mr. Gorin.

"Well, Hazel acted like the women on old black-and-white TV shows who can't do anything for themselves," she said. "If I were her, I wouldn't just sit there doing nothing, I'd act."

"What would you do?" asked Mr. Gorin.

"I'd do what Harrison did, I'd fight back."

"How?" asked Mr. Gorin, and proceeded to prod Savannah to explore her thoughts with subsequent prompts. When she had finished, Mr. Gorin reviewed the prompts he'd given and encouraged students to use such methods when leading their own discussions.

When the class completed their initial instruction in generating questions for "Harrison Bergeron," Mr. Gorin asked the students to form small groups to generate their own questions for another thematically-related short story, Twain's "The Man That Corrupted Hadleyburg." As he often did, Mr. Gorin allowed students to choose their own groups as long as they stayed productive. At times he had to break up groups that had difficulty maintaining their focus, but for the most part he found that self-selected groups were more cohesive than those that he formed according to his own interests. Mr. Gorin often had to defend his grouping practices to administrators who observed his classes because students often chose to work with students of the same race. He originally felt uncomfortable with this arrangement, but the alternatives made him feel even more uncomfortable. He had tried to distribute the minority students evenly among the groups, but found that in so doing he was singling them out, something that they clearly resented. As he looked at the make up of the groups that students chose, he saw that they all had a common denominator. In some cases it was race. In others they all had attended the same junior high. Other groups consisted entirely of athletes from the same sport. Some groups were all girls, others all boys. To make distinctions based on race but not on other factors seemed unfair to him, so he decided to let students pick their own partners regardless of how it might look to an outsider.

For this small-group activity he told each group that their job was to generate a set of questions for discussion-leading purposes. Mr. Gorin circulated around the room to listen to what students were saying as they generated their questions. As he eavesdropped on group discussions he heard a different type of conversation going on than typically took place during his teacher-led discussions. In order to generate their questions the students needed to talk about the story to determine which issues were important enough to explore with the class. Often several students spoke at once as they collaborated on generating questions, a spontaneity that Mr. Gorin often found lacking in formal class discussions. There was often laughter, colloquial speech, vociferous disagreement, and other facets of interaction that were generally absent from his teacher-led discussions. Early in the period he overheard one group as they worked on generating a textually explicit question:

> *Baxter:* OK, we've got to make up one of these questions that asks for some basic stated information, but we can't ask what the title of the story is.
>
> *Janet:* Well, it's about a man who corrupted a town called Hadleyburg by tempting everyone with money. Before that they'd always been good people. Maybe we could ask a question about the people of the town before the stranger came.
>
> *Randy:* What were they like before he came?
>
> *Cindy:* Well, let's see, it says right here at the beginning, "Hadleyburg was the most honest and upright town in all the region," so we could ask a question about that.
>
> *Randy:* Except one problem, they really weren't honest or upright, they just appeared to be. So how about, "What was the *reputation* of the people of Hadleyburg before the stranger came?"
>
> *Cindy:* Yeah, let's do that. . . .

Students settled on the explicit questions fairly easily. Their generation of inferential questions was more difficult. Mr. Gorin overheard another group trying to generate a complex-implied-relationship question; that is, one that asks about relationships that must be inferred from many different pieces of information. To do so they needed to discuss many parts of the story so that they could identify encompassing relationships from the story as a whole:

> *Teddy:* Okay, next we've got to do one of these complex-implied-relationship questions. What's that?

Students adjust their use of spoken, written, and visual language (e.g., conventions, style, vocabulary) to communicate effectively with a variety of audiences and for different purposes.

Students conduct research on issues and interests by generating ideas and questions, and by posing problems. They gather, evaluate, and synthesize data from a variety of sources (e.g., print and nonprint texts, artifacts, people) to communicate their discoveries in ways that suit their purpose and audience.

Kiki: I don't know. Hey, Mr. Gorin!

Mr. Gorin: Yes?

Kiki: What are we supposed to do for these complex-implied-whatever-
they-ares?

Mr. Gorin: Well, these aren't easy. To ask one of these you really have to
read the story carefully and try to think about things that aren't stated
directly, but that add up into one big truth about the story.

Tess: Could you do one for us?

Mr. Gorin: Well, I've already helped you with one. You give it a shot first,
and then let me know if you're still having trouble.

Tess: Well, it was worth a try. OK, what's this story about?

Karla: It's about a guy who went to this town and, like, made everybody corrupt.

Teddy: Right. Everybody thought they were upright at the beginning, but
became tempted by all the money and started plotting about how to get
it.

Kiki: Right. It *says* that everyone was upright, but you can tell that they really
aren't.

Tess: Like, where?

Kiki: Well, that first person who gets the money tells her husband, that Mr.
Richards guy, and he was like, "Well let's just keep that money and if the
stranger ever comes back, we can go, 'Forget you, we never saw you
before.'"

Teddy: Right, and everybody's like that. Everybody *appeared* to be good and
upright, but underneath it all they were just as greedy and mean as anybody else.

Tess: Yeah, and when they were talking about that preacher, that one guy
was like, hold on, let me find it, here it is, "Well, Burgess deserves it—he
will never get another congregation here. Mean as the town is, it knows
how to estimate *him*." So even the people in the town know that they're
kind of mean underneath their polite facade.

Kiki: Oh, nice word, facade.

Tess: Thanks.

Karla: Right, and that's just at the beginning when they think they're upright
and can't be corrupted. Or at least it appears on the surface that they
can't be corrupted. As the story goes on it just gets—

Kiki: Yeah, they just keep getting worse and worse, or, maybe, that's not it,
they—

Teddy: Right, they're not getting worse; it's just that they get more obvious.
You know, they're like, "That's my money, I must be the one who was
kind to the stranger," even though they were, like, really mean, and the
stranger actually wanted revenge, and so—

Tess: Yeah, so they're not really getting greedier, they're just showing it
more.

Karla: So, how are we supposed to ask a question about this?

Tess: I don't know. Let's see. What seems to be the thing that we're talking about? The people think they're upright, that they can't be corrupted, but they're already corrupt inside, and the stranger just tricks them into showing it more on the outside.

Teddy: Right, and at the end they change their motto so that it's honest and says that they *can* be led into temptation.

Karla: So what's the question we ask?

Kiki: Let's see, it's got to cover different parts of the story and be about something that's not stated directly. During the whole story everyone's really corrupt, but they've got a *facade* of being honest, but finally at the end everyone acts corrupt, and they're finally honest about being dishonest. How can we ask a question about that?

Teddy: This is like "Jeopardy," we know the answer but have to ask the question.

Kiki: [hums the "Jeopardy" theme song]

Tess: How about, "Are the people of Hadleyburg corrupt, or did the stranger corrupt them?"

Kiki: Well, that's close, but we're not supposed to ask questions that have yes/no answers. So we've got to try to say it differently.

Karla: How about if we use this question to try to ask about the corruption of the people throughout the story? Like this, "What did the man who corrupted Hadleyburg do to the people of Hadleyburg?"

Teddy: Wait, I have an idea. What would've happened if the stranger didn't tempt them? Maybe we could ask a question like that. "How corrupt would the people of Hadleyburg be if the stranger didn't lead them into temptation?"

Kiki: And delivered them from evil.

Teddy: To answer that, people would have to think about how corrupt the townspeople really are anyhow.

Tess: Yeah, but someone could answer that by going, like, "Really corrupt." So we'll have to ask more questions, like "Give examples from different parts of the story that show what you mean." That way they'll have to show that they understand how corrupt the characters are.

Kiki: Let's check with Mr. Gorin. Hey Mr. Gorin! . . .

The groups worked in this fashion, checking with Mr. Gorin when necessary and preparing both cognitive and affective questions for the story. After the groups were finished they exchanged their questions with another group and critiqued them to see if they met the criteria of each question type. Following the critiques, each group revised their questions and then exchanged them with a different group, this time for the purpose of responding to the questions, with the responses turned back to the original group for evaluation.

Following this initial instruction in generating and responding to questions, each group took responsibility for leading a discussion of a set of chapters from *Huckleberry Finn.* Each group had two days to prepare its questions. Although at times students appeared to be off-task, his monitoring of student progress revealed that their discussions were productive: students thought carefully about the chapters they were responsible for and related them to the rest of the novel, much as they had done for their discussions of "The Man That Corrupted Hadleyburg."

The actual student-led discussions provided an interesting contrast to normal classroom discourse. Each group knew that they needed their classmates' support for a successful discussion, and so tended to participate in other groups' discussions as part of their reciprocal dependency. The discussions covered a greater range of issues than were normally addressed. In the past Mr. Gorin had steered students away from discussing aspects of the novel that he felt sidetracked them from understanding the book's literary merit. When he removed himself from the discussion, however, the students often gravitated to the very issues he felt were trivial in grasping the novel's commentary on society.

One discussion-leading group consisted of three African American students, Andre, Sherice, and Emmitt, and one mixed-race student, Adrianna. They decided to start their discussion of Chapters 17–24, when Huck and Jim leave the Grangerfords and take up with the duke and dauphin, by posing one of the affective questions they had developed. Andre started by saying, "Have you ever been in a situation like the one Huck and Jim are in during these chapters? If so, how did you feel?"

Gregg, an African American student, immediately raised his hand and said, "Yes I have. I was thinking about that while I read the chapter. Some of this stuff really got me. Let me find one part. . . . Look at page 101. Let me read you what it says:

> Each person had their own nigger to wait on them—Buck too. My nigger had a monstrous easy time, because I warn't use to having anybody do anything for me, but Buck's was on the jump most of the time.
>
> This was all there was of the family now, but there used to be more—three sons; they got killed; and Emmeline that died.
>
> The old gentleman owned a lot of farms and over a hundred niggers.

"Well, you're asking me how I feel about this book, and I don't feel so good. I feel the way I feel at work. All the bosses are white and they act like we're their niggers. I feel like Buck's slave because my boss keeps me on the jump, more than he does the white boys who work there."

"Could you please elaborate?" asked Sherice.

"I'd be happy to elaborate. I hate the way Huck keeps calling Jim a nigger. I've been called nigger all my life, and I don't see why I have to come to school and see black people called niggers in the books we read. How come we never read books by black writers where they call white people 'honkeys' on every page?"

Mike, a white student who'd grown up in Iron City, raised his hand. "Now wait a minute. You black people call each other nigger all the time. What do you expect us to do? Even in this book Jim calls blacks niggers. So I think it's just the way it is. Besides, it's just a name. Why can't you just read the book and learn from it?"

Sherice responded, "Well, it's not just a name. And it's different when black people and white people say nigger. How'd you feel if I called you a redneck? You'd get pretty mad, wouldn't you? But you call your friends rednecks and laugh because you're proud of it. It's the same thing."

"Well," said Mike, "if I had to read books where the white people were called rednecks, I wouldn't sit around crying about it, I'd just read the book."

Adrianna broke in. "Mike, how did you feel about these chapters?"

Students adjust their use of spoken, written, and visual language (e.g., conventions, style, vocabulary) to communicate effectively with a variety of audiences and for different purposes.

Students apply a wide range of strategies to comprehend, interpret, evaluate, and appreciate texts. They draw on their prior experience, their interactions with other readers and writers, their knowledge of word meaning and other texts, their word identification strategies, and their understanding of textual features (e.g., sound-letter correspondence, sentence structure, context, graphics).

Students develop an understanding of and respect for diversity in language use, patterns, and dialects across cultures, ethnic groups, geographic regions, and social roles.

"How'd I feel? I didn't feel nothin'. It's a good story, it's entertaining, our teacher told us to read it, this is school, so I read it. What's there to feel? It's a book, not real life."

Emmitt decided to improvise with a new question. "Does anyone think Mark Twain is a racist? My dad does. He's very mad about us reading this book."

Lexie, a white girl, responded. "I don't think he's racist. Jim's the only decent character in the whole book. Even Huck's kind of a jerk. And everybody they meet on land is a loser. Huck's the one who's a racist. Mark Twain only wrote the book. I think if he was a racist then he'd make Jim look immoral or something. Jim's ignorant, but then he didn't have an education or anything. But he's a good person."

A black student named Carol spoke up. "It doesn't matter to me which one's the racist. There's plenty of racists in this world, and a few more won't make a difference. What I don't like is having to read them in school. I thought that school was supposed to make everybody equal, but I don't see no equality here. Jim's the first black character we've seen in a book all year, and he's an ignorant slave, saying 'I'ze gwine ketch up wid dem niggers' and other such stuff that makes black folks look like fools. I think it's the school that's racist, and that's what I don't like."

The discussion continued, with students addressing social issues that formed the context of their reading in a way that Mr. Gorin had always discouraged. It was often tense, and the issues were not resolved at the end of the period; while Mr. Gorin had always striven to reach "closure" in his discussions, students exited the class still arguing about the issues with some intensity. He found much of the discussion unsettling, and was somewhat discouraged by the degree of dissatisfaction he learned about through the students' contributions. Yet he also saw the novel from a different perspective than he previously had, understanding better how it could engender a negative reaction with some readers.

While not all of the student-led discussions resulted in such heated exchanges about the merit of the book, they did allow students to use their own histories as frameworks for constructing meaning for the characters and their experiences. Mr. Gorin decided to open up their writing opportunities as well, allowing them to use the material from class discussions in their graded responses. In previous years he had clearly circumscribed students' writing opportunities, limiting them to formal analysis of the novel. As he listened to the student-led discussions, he jotted down ideas on how students could fruitfully compose texts that helped them develop meaningful responses to the novel. He presented students with a number of possibilities, from which they could make a choice. Students could do any two of the following:

1. Keep a journal in response to their reading and discussion of the novel.
2. Participate in the community-wide discussion of curriculum and instruction by writing a letter to the school board, English department chair, student newspaper, and/or community newspaper expressing a position on why *Huckleberry Finn* should or should not be included in the literature curriculum.
3. Write a conventional analysis on some aspect of *Huckleberry Finn*.
4. Produce a narration or other creative work that is related to some aspect of *Huckleberry Finn*. It could be a satire of social folly within the school or community, a narrative about race relations, or other thematically related original work.

Students conduct research on issues and interests by generating ideas and questions, and by posing problems. They gather, evaluate, and synthesize data from a variety of sources (e.g., print and nonprint texts, artifacts, people) to communicate their discoveries in ways that suit their purpose and audience.

Students read a wide range of literature from many periods in many genres to build an understanding of the many dimensions (e.g., philosophical, ethical, aesthetic) of human experience.

Students employ a wide range of strategies as they write and use different writing process elements appropriately to communicate with different audiences for a variety of purposes.

Adrianna, intrigued by the parallels among "The Man That Corrupted Hadleyburg," *The Adventures of Huckleberry Finn,* and the tensions present in Lafayette Heights, wrote the following satire:

The Woman That Corrupted Lafayette Heights

Once there was a town called Lafayette Heights. People there were happy, and no one could corrupt them. There were people of all different colors and backgrounds but they all got along very well, or so it seemed.

But there was a woman who'd passed through town long ago (which color she was, it didn't matter). Someone had done her wrong, and she wanted to get back at the whole town. So she took a copy of *Huckleberry Finn* and left it in the English department of the high school with a note that said if all the teachers used it she'd make the school rich. The principal liked this idea and so ordered all of the teachers to teach this novel.

Students read it and so did their parents. Some thought that it was a very fine book because it showed how greedy and selfish people are and taught them lessons about life. These people thought anyone who read *Huckleberry Finn* would become smarter and more moral, which would be quite a trick in a very moral town like Lafayette Heights.

Other people didn't like the book so much because it used words that harmed them. These people didn't like the way Huck Finn thought black people were inferior and called them "niggers." They started complaining about the book and saying that people shouldn't have to read racist feelings in school.

All of the happy people in Lafayette Heights weren't so happy anymore. They began fighting about this book and calling each other racists and arguing about what kinds of books people should have to read in school. Nobody could agree on what to do, and nobody liked the situation the way it was. They all wanted to go back to the way things used to be when everyone was happy, but it was too late.

Then one day the townspeople got a letter from the woman who'd started the whole mess. The note said,

Dear People of Lafayette Heights,
    I promised that I'd make the school rich if you read this book. Now that you see each other for what you really are, you are richer for it.
    Sincerely,
    An Old Friend

These choices enabled students to have some say in how they made sense of the novel and their discussions. They also had some say in who would read and respond to their efforts. Some students wanted only Mr. Gorin to read their writing, since they were exploring highly sensitive ideas and feelings; some students had racially-charged views that they did not want to make public, yet which they shared with him for both academic credit and to receive his personal response. Other students wished to join the public fray and used their writing as the basis for public expressions of their views. Adrianna, for instance, both sent her satire to the school paper, which published it, and submitted it to the school's annual writing competition.

The students' writing was far more emotional than most of the writing that Mr. Gorin's students had done for him in the past, and created discomfort for him with some faculty members who did not want to encourage students to begin questioning the curriculum any more than they already did, especially through such public media as the local newspaper or school board meetings. Yet he saw a conviction in their writing that exceeded most of their previous

Students participate as knowledgeable, reflective, creative, and critical members of a variety of literacy communities.

efforts and so decided that whatever dissonance his students' expressions caused with his own sensibilities or the community's would be productive in the long run.

The unit on *Huckleberry Finn* was in many ways excruciating for Mr. Gorin. The discussions on the novel ranged far from those that he had led in the past, when his own questions had limited the topics that students could discuss in relation to it. He worried that the focus on students' affective response to the novel came at the expense to their understanding of the literary conventions of irony that he believed justified the inclusion of *Huckleberry Finn* in the curriculum and absolved Mark Twain of blame for the racist views expressed by the characters in the novel. Yet he also saw greater student involvement in the discussions, greater investment in the issues explored, and a quantum leap in their ability to pose questions that helped them inquire into the parts of the novel that they found worth pursuing. While often going beyond the range of issues specifically raised by Twain, the discussions were sufficiently grounded in the text itself to satisfy Mr. Gorin that they were not ignoring the novel in order to talk about unrelated issues.

The unit caused Mr. Gorin to rethink some aspects of his teaching. His African American students' consistent observation that their voice was excluded from the curriculum caused him to look for ways to include more works by black authors and to present a case for curriculum revision to his colleagues. He also liked the way his students ran their own discussions and decided that by teaching students to ask questions earlier in the year, he could plan more such opportunities and thus encourage more rigorous student inquiry than he'd been able to achieve in the past.

He felt that the writing that students did in response to the novel had mixed results. In previous years he had led the whole class through a specific set of steps in learning how to produce a specific type of writing, such as an argument about an interpretation, an extended definition of a concept such as hypocrisy and subsequent analysis of the novel in terms of that definition, or some other type of writing that followed a given set of conventions. By allowing students choice he was less directive in how they interpreted the story. However, he was also less helpful to them in their composing because he could not possibly teach ten different genres at once. He saw a need for both clear instruction in writing conventions and student choice in writing genres. Figuring out how to balance the two, however, would complicate his teaching in the years to come.

Standards in Practice

Mr. Gorin's students read and consider a classic of American literature, *The Adventures of Huckleberry Finn,* in a way that engages them in an exploration of the different perspectives people may take on the novel given their cultural experiences. To understand both their own response to the novel and that of others, students need to think about the relationship between the book's aesthetic merit and the moral dimensions of their response to it. In doing so they need to try to recognize both the ironic structure of the text and the emotional impact that irony can have on people whose negative experiences are being satirized. Students learn how to pose questions of three main types in order to learn procedures for inquiry in their subsequent reading and discussion of literature, in the process learning to generate ideas, questions, and problems to pursue in their thinking and writing. Although some students in this class are unlikely to develop empathy for the experiences of their classmates, they do make an effort to articulate their own perspectives on social relations and how these perspectives are represented in the novel. By sharing their writing with readerships outside the classroom, some students participate in a variety of literacy communities. Those students who are willing to listen to others have the potential to use their reading, writing, and discussion to develop and pursue goals for critical, aesthetic, and moral development.

Resources

Teaching Students of Other Races

Books and Articles

Bowers, C. A. (1991). *Culturally responsive teaching and supervision: A handbook for staff development.* New York: Teachers College Press.

Cazden, C. B., John, V. P., & Hymes, D. (Eds.). (1972). *Functions of language in the classroom.* New York: Teachers College Press.

Delpit, L. (1995). *Other people's children: Cultural conflict in the classroom.* New York: The New Press.

Fox, H. (1994). *Listening to the world: Cultural issues in academic writing.* Urbana, IL: National Council of Teachers of English.

Gilmore, P., & Glatthorn, A. A. (Eds.). (1982). *Children in and out of school: Ethnography and education.* Washington, D.C.: Center for Applied Linguistics.

Greenfield, P. M., & Cocking, R. R. (Eds.). (1994). *Cross-cultural roots of minority child development.* Hillsdale, NJ: L. Erlbaum Associates.

Hiebert, E. H. (Ed.). (1991). *Literacy for a diverse society: Perspectives, practices, and policies.* New York: Teachers College Press.

Krater, J., Zeni, J., & Cason, N. D. (1994). *Mirror images: Teaching writing in black and white.* Portsmouth, NH: Heinemann.

McIntosh, P. (1988). *White privilege and male privilege: A personal account of coming to see correspondences through work in women's studies.* Wellesley, MA: Wellesley College, Center for Research on Women.

Mitchell, C., & Weiler, K. (Eds.). (1991). *Rewriting literacy: Culture and the discourse of the other.* New York: Bergin & Garvey.

Morris, L. (Ed.). (1978). *Extracting learning styles from social/cultural diversity: A study of five American minorities.* Southwest Teacher Corps Network.

Scollon, R., & Scollon, S. B. K. (1981). *Narrative, literacy, and face in interethnic communication.* Norwood, NJ: Ablex Publishing Corp.

Smagorinsky, P. (1992). Towards a civic education in a multicultural society: Ethical problems in teaching literature. *English Education, 24*(4), 212–228.

Tobach, E., & Rogoff, B. (Eds.). (1994). *Challenging racism and sexism: Alternatives to genetic explanations.* New York: Feminist Press.

Trimmer, J., & Warnock, T. (Eds.). (1992). *Understanding others: Cultural and cross-cultural studies and the teaching of literature.* Urbana, IL: National Council of Teachers of English.

Weis, L. (1985). *Between two worlds: Black students in an urban community college.* Boston: Routledge & Kegan Paul.

Journals

Anthropology and Education Quarterly, American Anthropological Association, Arlington, VA

Cross-Cultural Research, Sage Publications

Hispanic Journal of Behavioral Sciences, Sage Publications

Journal of Black Psychology, Sage Publications

Journal of Black Studies, Sage Publications

Journal of Cross-Cultural Psychology, Sage Publications

Cognitive Taxonomies

Books and Articles

Bloom, B. (Ed.). (1956). *Taxonomy of educational objectives: The classification of educational goals* (Handbook 1: Cognitive Domain). New York: D. McKay.

Hillocks, G., Jr. (1980). Toward a hierarchy of skills in the comprehension of literature. *English Journal, 69*(3), 54–59.

Pearson, P. D., & Johnson, D. D. (1978). *Teaching reading comprehension.* New York: Holt, Rinehart & Winston.

Affect in the Curriculum

Books

Beane, J. A. (1990). *Affect in the curriculum: Toward democracy, dignity, and diversity.* New York: Teachers College Press.

Belenky, M. F., Clinchy, B. M., Goldberger, N. R., & Tarule, J. M. (1986). *Women's ways of knowing.* New York: Basic Books.

Bleich, D. (1975). *Reading and feelings.* Urbana, IL: National Council of Teachers of English.

Bogdan, D. (1992). *Re-educating the imagination: Toward a poetics, politics, and pedagogy of literary engagement.* Portsmouth, NH: Boynton/Cook Publishers.

Bruner, J. (1986). *Actual minds, possible worlds.* Cambridge, MA: Harvard University Press.

Clark, M. S., & Fiske, S. T. (Eds.). (1982). *Affect and cognition: The Seventeenth Annual Carnegie Symposium on Cognition.* Hillsdale, NJ: L. Erlbaum Associates.

Dewey, J. (1963). *Experience and education.* New York: Collier Books. (Original work published in 1938.)

Gilligan, C. (1982). *In a different voice: Psychological theory and women's development.* Cambridge, MA: Harvard University Press.

Hyson, M. C. (1994). *The emotional development of young children: Building an emotion-centered curriculum.* New York: Teachers College Press.

Langland, E., & Gove, W. (Eds.). (1983). *A feminist perspective in the academy: The difference it makes.* Chicago: University of Chicago Press.

Martin, J. R. (1992). *The schoolhome: Rethinking schools for changing families.* Cambridge, MA: Harvard University Press.

Martin, J. R. (1994). *Changing the educational landscape: Philosophy, women, and curriculum.* New York: Routledge.

Montessori, M. (1972). *Education and peace.* Chicago: Regnery.

Noddings, N. (1984). *Caring: A feminist approach to ethics and moral education.* Berkeley: University of California Press.

Noddings, N. (1992). *The challenge to care in schools: An alternative approach to education.* New York: Teachers College Press.

Rogers, C. (1969). *Freedom to learn: A view of what education might become.* Columbus, OH: Charles E. Merrill.

Valett, R. E. (1974). *Affective-humanistic education: Goals, programs, and learning activities.* Belmont, CA: Fearon.

Questioning

Books and Articles

Couch, L. (1989). Questioning our way to "Wisdom, Wonder, and Serendipitous Knowledge." *English Education, 21*(4), 230–238.

Dillon, J. T. (1982). The effect of questions in education and other enterprises. *Journal of Curriculum Studies, 14*(2), 127–152.

Dillon, J. T. (1983). *Teaching and the art of questioning.* Bloomington, IN: Phi Delta Kappa Educational Foundation.

Dillon, J. T. (1988). *Questioning and discussion: A multidisciplinary study.* Norwood, NJ: Ablex Publishing Corp.

Dillon, J. T. (1988). *Questioning and teaching: A manual of practice.* New York: Teachers College Press.

Dillon, J. T. (1988). The remedial status of student questioning. *Journal of Curriculum Studies, 20*(3), 197–210.

Dillon, J. T. (1990). *The practice of questioning.* New York: Routledge.

Farrar, M. T. (1986). Teacher questions: The complexity of the cognitively simple. *Instructional Science, 15*(2), 89–107.

Gall, M. D. (1970). The use of questions in teaching. *Review of Educational Research, 40,* 707–721.

Stotsky, S. (1986). Asking questions about ideas: A critical component in critical thinking. *The Leaflet, 35*(3), journal of the New England Association of Teachers of English.

Strother, D. (1989). Developing thinking skills through questioning. *Phi Delta Kappan, 71*(4), 324–370.

Wilen, W. W. (Ed.). (1987). *Questions, questioning techniques, and effective teaching.* Washington, D.C.: National Education Association.

Wilen, W. W. (1987). *Questioning skills, for teachers* (2nd ed.). Washington, D.C.: National Education Association.

Wilen, W. W. (Ed.). (1990). *Teaching and learning through discussion: The theory, research, and practice of the discussion method.* Springfield, IL: Charles C. Thomas.

Transactional Theories of Literary Response

Books

Anderson, P. M., & Rubano, G. (1991). *Enhancing aesthetic reading and response.* Urbana, IL: National Council of Teachers of English.

Andrasick, K. D. (1990). *Opening texts: Using writing to teach literature.* Portsmouth, NH: Heinemann.

Applebee, A. N. (1993). *Literature in the secondary school: Studies of curriculum and instruction in the United States.* NCTE Research Report No. 25. Urbana, IL: National Council of Teachers of English.

Beach, R. (1993). *A teacher's introduction to reader-response theories.* Urbana, IL: National Council of Teachers of English.

Beach, R., & Marshall, J. (1991). *Teaching literature in the secondary school.* San Diego: Harcourt Brace Jovanovich.

Corcoran, B., & Evans, E. (1987). *Readers, texts, teachers.* Upper Montclair, NJ: Boynton/Cook Publishers.

Farrell, E. J., & Squire, J. R. (1990). *Transactions with literature: A fifty-year perspective.* Urbana, IL: National Council of Teachers of English.

Hynds, S. (1994). *Making connections: Language and learning in the classroom.* Norwood, MA: Christopher-Gordon Publishers, Inc.

Langer, J. A. (Ed.). (1992). *Literature instruction: A focus on student response.* Urbana, IL: National Council of Teachers of English.

Nelms, B. F. (Ed.). (1988). *Literature in the classroom: Readers, texts, and contexts.* Urbana, IL: National Council of Teachers of English.

Newell, G. E., & Durst, R. K. (Eds.). (1993). *Exploring texts: The role of discussion and writing in the teaching and learning of literature.* Norwood, MA: Christopher-Gordon Publishers, Inc.

Phelan, P. (Ed.). (1990). *Literature and life: Making connections in the classroom. Classroom practices in teaching English, Vol. 25.* Urbana, IL: National Council of Teachers of English.

Probst, R. E. (1988). *Response and analysis: Teaching literature in junior and senior high school years.* Portsmouth, NH: Heinemann.

Purves, A., Rogers, T., & Soter, A. (1990). *How porcupines make love II: Teaching a response centered literature curriculum.* New York: Longman.

Rosenblatt, L. M. (1978). *The reader, the text, the poem: The transactional theory of the literary work.* Carbondale, IL: Southern Illinois University Press.

Rosenblatt, L. M. (1983). *Literature as exploration* (3rd ed.). New York: The Language Association of America.

Simmons, J. S., & Deluzain, H. E. (1992). *Teaching literature in the middle and secondary grades.* Boston: Allyn & Bacon.

Squire, J. (1964). *The responses of adolescents while reading four short stories.* Champaign, IL: National Council of Teachers of English.

Sullivan, J., & Hurley, J. (1982). *Teaching literature inductively.* Anaheim, CA: Canterbury.

Vine, H. A., & Faust, M. A. (1993). *Situating readers: Students making meaning of literature.* Urbana, IL: National Council of Teachers of English.

Wilhelm, J. (in press). *Developing readers: Teaching engaged and reflective reading with adolescents.* New York: Teachers College Press.

Journals

Journal of Reading, International Reading Association

Journal of Reading Behavior, National Reading Conference

Reader, Michigan Technological University

Readerly/Writerly Texts: Essays on Literature, Literary/Textual Criticism, and Pedagogy, Eastern New Mexico University

Reading Psychology, Taylor and Frances
Reading Research Quarterly, International Reading Association
The Reading Teacher, International Reading Association
Research in the Teaching of English, National Council of Teachers of English
Voices from the Middle, National Council of Teachers of English

E-mail Network

This is the address of Litnet, based at the Center for the Teaching and Learning of Literature: listproc@itc.org

Reflective Teaching

Books

Casey, K. (1993). *I answer with my life: Life histories of women teachers working for social change.* New York: Routledge.

Connelly, F. M., & Clandinin, D. J. (1988). *Teachers as curriculum planners: Narratives of experience.* New York: Teachers College Press.

Cutuly, J. (1993). *Home of the wildcats: Perils of an English teacher.* Urbana, IL: National Council of Teachers of English.

Gere, A. R., Fairbanks, C., Howes, A., Roop, L., & Schaafsma, D. (1992). *Language and reflection: An integrated approach to teaching English.* New York: Maxwell Macmillan International.

Grimmett, P., & Erickson, G. (Eds.). (1988). *Reflection in teacher education.* New York: Teachers College Press.

Grossman, P. L. (1990). *The making of a teacher: Teacher knowledge and teacher education.* New York: Teachers College Press.

Handal, G., & Lauvas, P. (1987). *Promoting reflective teaching: Supervision in practice.* Philadelphia, PA: Open University Press.

Hillocks, G., Jr. (1995). *Teaching writing as reflective practice.* New York: Teachers College Press.

Larson, R., & McCracken, T. (in press). *Teaching college English and English education.* Urbana, IL: National Council of Teachers of English.

Rose, M. (1989). *Lives on the boundary: The struggles and achievements of America's underprepared.* New York: Free Press.

Schön, D. (1983). *The reflective practitioner: How professionals think in action.* New York: Basic Books.

Schön, D. (1987). *Educating the reflective practitioner: Toward a new design for teaching and learning in the professions.* San Francisco: Jossey-Bass.

Schön, D. (Ed.). (1991). *The reflective turn: Case studies in and on educational practice.* New York: Teachers College Press.

Tabachnick, B. R., & Zeichner, K. M. (Eds.). (1991). *Issues and practices in inquiry-oriented teacher education.* New York: Falmer.

Villanueva, V. (1993). *Bootstraps: From an American academic of color.* Urbana, IL: National Council of Teachers of English.

Classroom Discourse

Books

Barnes, D., Britton, J., & Rosen, H. (Eds.). (1969). *Language, the learner, and the school.* Baltimore, MD: Penguin Books.

Bauman, R., & Sherzer, J. (Eds.). (1974). *Explorations in the ethnography of speaking.* New York: Cambridge University Press.

Bellack, A., Kleibard, H., Hyman, R., & Smith, F. (1966). *The language of the classroom.* New York: Teachers College Press.

Cazden, C. B. (1988). *Classroom discourse: The language of teaching and learning.* Portsmouth, NH: Heinemann.

Cazden, C. B. (1992). *Whole language plus: Essays on literacy in the United States and New Zealand.* New York: Teachers College Press.

Cazden, C. B., John, V., & Hymes, D. (Eds.). (1972). *Functions of language in the classroom.* New York: Teachers College Press.

Hynds, S., & Rubin, D. L. (Eds.). (1990). *Perspectives on talk and learning.* Urbana, IL: National Council of Teachers of English.

Marshall, J. D., Smagorinsky, P., & Smith, M. W. (1995). *The language of interpretation: Patterns of discourse in discussions of literature.* NCTE Research Report No. 27. Urbana, IL: National Council of Teachers of English.

Mehan, H. (1979). *Learning lessons.* Cambridge: Harvard University Press.

Nystrand, M. (in press). *Dialogic instruction: A study of the social mediation of understanding and learning in eighth- and ninth-grade literature instruction.* New York: Teachers College Press.

Tannen, D. (1991). *You just don't understand: Women and men in conversation.* New York: Ballantine.

Journals

Communication Education, Speech Communication Association

Communication Monographs, Speech Communication Association

Communication Research, Sage Publications

Discourse Processes, Ablex Publishing Corporation

Human Communication Research, Sage Publications

Journal of Communication, University of Pennsylvania and Oxford University Press

Linguistics and Education, Ablex Publishing Corporation

Text: An Interdisciplinary Journal for the Study of Discourse, Mouton, Inc.

Chapter Three

Tales of the Prairie

Eddie Gomez taught in Prairie View, a small ranching community in the vast plains of the American Midwest. People entering Prairie View travelled a two-lane state highway through miles of crops and pastureland before slowing to 25 MPH in the downtown area. After weaving through a group of white clapboard churches on the edge of town, the road passed by the post office, diner, gas station, barbershop, and other small businesses that provided the center of commerce in Prairie View. The highway next wound through a small residential section consisting of one-story homes and trailers, then quickly resumed its normal speed as it curved through the ranches and farms that rolled across the prairie.

> At present the honey-bee swarms in myriads, in the noble groves and forests which skirt and intersect the prairies, and extend along the alluvial bottoms of the rivers. It seems to me as if these beautiful regions answer literally to the description of the land of promise, "a land flowing with milk and honey"; for the rich pasturage of the prairies is calculated to sustain herds of cattle as countless as the sands upon the sea-shore, while the flowers with which they are enamelled render them a very paradise for the nectar-seeking bee.
>
> Washington Irving, *A Tour on the Prairies*, pp. 50–51.

The town's school system was consolidated in a small cluster of buildings just off the main street near the downtown area, next to the rodeo arena that provided the summer's biggest social event. The school grounds were spacious, providing ample room for the football stadium where every fall the pride of Prairie View did battle under the Friday night lights. On the edge of the business district stood the cotton warehouse that bustled with delivery trucks during the late fall harvest, leaving downtown and roadbeds speckled with tufts of white. The middle and high schools shared the same faculty; Mr. Gomez was one of two English teachers serving grades 8–12. He taught two classes of eighth graders, two of ninth, and one of twelfth. A typical class size was fifteen to eighteen students, including those who repeated courses, with graduating classes typically numbering about twenty-five.

Most students in Prairie View came from families involved in ranching and farming. The school provided short vacations and very few holidays during the school year, and many students used the long summers to work on their family ranches and farms. Families who did not work the land often provided support services such as feed, fertilizer, and grain, or worked at the post office, diner, or other small businesses in town.

Other people settled in Prairie View for its quality of life, especially for children. Among such families one parent often worked away from home during the week in distant oil fields or other regional businesses. Although the vast spaces of the ranches often physically separated residents from one another, a closeness in the personal relations among townspeople bound them together—doors were rarely locked at night, neighbors helped one another in times of stress, and a general feeling of friendliness and common cause permeated Prairie View's social life.

Many students at Prairie View High School, while immersed in agricultural life, were well connected to the world at large. From the road, satellite dishes were visible outside the houses on many of the ranches, bringing MTV, international broadcasts, and the world beyond into their lives. While country and western music played in the background of the barbershop, diner, and their parents' pickup trucks, students were just as likely to blast current rock music through the headphones of their portable cassette players. The Internet and fax connections that were important to modern farming also gave many Prairie View students access to cyberspace, providing them with a broad range of perspectives through which to construct their world.

Not all students came from land-owning families. Some were the children of ranch hands who lived in modest on-site housing provided by the ranchers for a percentage of their wages. The town's inhabitants included Mexican American and Native American residents who made up about 15% of the total population. Some of these minority residents owned their own ranches; others either worked as ranch hands or owned or worked in one of the downtown area's small businesses.

Mr. Gomez, like several other faculty members, had originally lived in the "teacherage," a small set of rudimentary cottages just off school grounds provided for teachers to compensate for the low salary paid by the district, which had little industrial tax base to draw on to support its schools. After marrying he'd bought a home in a small residential area just off Prairie View's business district. Other members of the primarily female faculty lived on farms or ranches, often spending time each day before and after school helping to operate the family business.

The community as a whole reflected the masculine dominance of frontier and ranching life. Men occupied most decision-making positions in town governance and school administration. Mr. Gomez was one of the few men on the faculty. Like the other male teachers, he coached a sport during the fall, winter, and spring, and also in the summer evening programs.

The school's limited resources and small student body mitigated against providing expansive services for students. The school provided few classes in art, music, or foreign languages, although there was an extracurricular band program for students who played at football and basketball games. The school provided no drama productions, debating team, or book clubs. The primary extracurricular activities were sports, Future Homemakers of America, Future Farmers of America, and the 4-H Club. The classes most highly valued by the community were those that taught skills needed for farm and ranch life: science, math, vocational agriculture, and home economics. The school library was the only library in town. To buy a book, someone from Prairie View needed to drive across the county to a chain department store that stocked a small display of bestsellers. The students who went to college tended to major in agriculture in order to run the family farm more efficiently. Some students had ambitions to move to the city following graduation or to go to college "away from home"—that is, to a college in a different part of the state—to get a different view of life. Most students, though, stayed in town following high school graduation, preferring the friendliness and familiarity of Prairie View to the faster pace, claustrophobia, and impersonal social relations of larger towns and cities.

> Ours was just another one of those little towns, I guess, about a thousand or so people, where everybody knows everybody else; and on your way to the post office, you'd nod and speak to so many friends that your neck would be rubbed raw when you went in to get your mail if there was any. It took you just about an hour to get up through town, say hello, talk over the late news, family gossip, sickness, weather, crops, and lousy politics. Everybody had something to say about something, or somebody, and you usually knew almost word for word what it was going to be about before you heard them say it, as we had well-known and highly expert talkers on all subjects in and out of this world.
>
> Woody Guthrie, *Bound for Glory,* p. 37.

Students, like older community members, spoke in a rural drawl and dialect. Around town it was common to hear people say, "She ain't doin' nothin' about it," or "I might could help y'all out on that," or "It don't look like it's fixin' to rain none." Even many school faculty, administrators, and board members—most of whom had grown up in either Prairie View or towns in the region—were known to speak colloquially both in and out of the classroom. Though most townspeople spoke in a rural dialect, the primary emphasis in the English curriculum was on formal grammar. The focus on grammar stemmed from both local values and from broader social and economic pressures. At the community level, the emphasis on grammar spoke pragmatically to community values and needs, more so than would a focus on other strands of the language arts curriculum. The selections in the school's state-loaned literature anthology seemed quite remote from the students' agricultural world; few students or parents found *Macbeth* and other stalwarts of the curriculum to be helpful in growing crops during a drought, getting a good price on cattle, or stopping the fullback on third and short. Many parents were more concerned that their children could read instructions on how to repair machinery or write a business letter regarding the purchase of farm equipment than that they could read Chaucer or write an analysis of *The Scarlet Letter.*

The emphasis on grammar—which according to the Prairie View curriculum included attention to all aspects of language knowledge and usage covered in their grammar textbook—was also a function of dictates imposed by the state. School effectiveness was assessed by state-mandated standardized tests, and ineffective schools were ordered to close and consolidate with a neighboring district that met the state's minimum requirements. The language arts assessment included a test of formal grammar, including labeling parts of speech, correcting poorly punctuated sentences, and identifying incorrect usage of verbs, pronouns, homonyms, and so on. If students did poorly on this test in conjunction with a writing assessment and tests in other subject areas, Prairie View would be forced to close its schools and consolidate with the nearby Antelope Hills schools, their historical rivals in sports that typically had acceptable test scores.

"I ain't no plumb whole stranger; mama cat knowed me when I wuz jest a little teeny weeny baby; jest this long; an' my mama had ta keep me all nice an' warm jest like them little baby cats, so's I wouldn't freeze, so's nothin' wouldn't git me."

Woody Guthrie, *Bound for Glory,* pp. 74–75.

Like many other small towns across the country, Prairie View derived much of its identity from its school system. School events and church functions provided the axis of social life for residents of Prairie View, and provided historical ties to the past and the foundation for the future. Along with the churches, the schools were the most venerable institutions of the town and were inviolate in the minds of the townspeople. While Wednesday nights and Sundays were devoted to church, much of the rest of the week revolved around school. The high school football and basketball games brought the whole town together to root for the Prairie View Hawks. The students who wore the Hawks uniform were the pride of the community and were celebrities among students, teachers, and adults alike. The stands at the home football and basketball games were filled with townspeople cheering for the Hawks, and many Prairie View residents drove the two-lane country roads to support the teams at away games as well. The schools and children, epitomized in the minds of many Prairie View people by the sports teams, often served as the focal point for their celebration of the present and hopes for the future. Closing the high school and shipping the community's children off to another town would result in a loss that Prairie View might never recover from. Emphasizing grammar, therefore, was a way of preserving a cultural institution and maintaining continuity and stability in a part of the country where the vicissitudes of nature and the economy often made the survival of families and communities perilous.

Mr. Gomez himself had grown up in a neighboring community, the son of Mexican immigrants who had been the cook and ranch hand for a large cattle ranch. Throughout his youth and teens he had worked the ranch with his brothers and sisters. However, unlike most kids he grew up with, he did not aspire to ride rodeo or work on a ranch; he went to the nearby regional state university and after his sophomore year decided to become a teacher. In order to succeed academically and get strong recommendations from his college professors when applying for teaching jobs, Mr. Gomez needed to learn standard English. While appreciating the beauty and utility of the rural dialect he'd grown up speaking, he recognized that it provided limited employment opportunities for adults if they should leave Prairie View. As a teacher, Mr. Gomez was often torn between his understanding of how the colloquial English of Prairie View residents served them well in community affairs and was sufficient for the career goals of his students within Prairie View and similar communities, and his understanding of how it provided career barriers if the local dialect remained the only linguistic choice available to them.

[I]n Roadville and Trackton the different ways children learned to use language were dependent on the ways in which each community structured their families, defined the roles that community members could assume, and played out their concepts of childhood that guided child socialization. In addition, for each group, the place of religious activities was inextricably linked to the valuation of language in determining an individual's access to goods, services, and estimations of position and power in the community. In communities throughout the world, these and other features of the cultural milieu affect the ways in which children learn to use language. The place of language in the cultural life of each social group is interdependent with the habits and values of behaving shared among members of that group.

Shirley Brice Heath, *Ways with Words*, p. 11.

Mr. Gomez found the grammatical emphasis of his school's curriculum to be problematic. On the one hand, it served his goal of helping students develop conventional syntax to supplement their native rural tongue. On the other hand, Prairie View's approach to teaching grammar was so heavily oriented to isolated drill of the parts of speech that it seemed unproductive in actually providing students with linguistic alternatives that they could appropriately use. From his own experiences, Mr. Gomez believed in developing multiple dialects to serve different communicative needs, both those that are immediately necessary and those that could provide greater opportunities in the future. Yet he was frustrated because using the approach taken by his grammar book to teach students about the standard language was ineffective and often counterproductive. It did not change his students' use of language in either their speech or writing, and often made them hostile to the subject area that he so passionately felt they needed to learn. His colleagues believed that the ineffectiveness of grammar instruction could only be solved by *increasing* the amount of time spent on labeling the parts of speech and diagramming sentences. Mr. Gomez felt that this strategy would only further exacerbate the problems he found with traditional approaches to teaching grammar.

> [I]n view of the widespread agreement of research studies based on many types of students and teachers, the conclusion can be stated in strong and unqualified terms: the teaching of formal grammar has a negligible or, because it usually displaces some instruction and practice in actual composition, even a harmful effect on the improvement of writing.
>
> Richard Braddock, Richard Lloyd-Jones, & Lowell Schoer, *Research in Written Composition*, pp. 37–38.

Mr. Gomez sought ways to teach students about language that were tied to their interests and also tied to other strands of the curriculum, such as literature, writing, and oral speech. After years of frustration in trying to teach grammar according to the textbook, he saw an opportunity with his ninth graders to integrate instruction across the strands of the curriculum so that students could learn to appreciate the vitality and appropriateness of their native dialect and also learn functions of language that enabled consonance with more mainstream speakers.

> The study of traditional school grammar (i.e., the definition of parts of speech, the parsing of sentences, etc.) has no effect on raising the quality of student writing. Every other focus of instruction examined in this review is stronger. Taught in certain ways, grammar and mechanics instruction has a deleterious effect on student writing. In some studies a heavy emphasis on mechanics and usage (e.g., marking every error) resulted in significant losses in overall quality. School boards, administrators, and teachers who impose the systematic study of traditional school grammar on their students over lengthy periods of time in the name of teaching writing do them a gross disservice which should not be tolerated by anyone concerned with the effective teaching of good writing. We need to learn how to teach standard usage and mechanics after careful task analysis and with minimal grammar.
>
> George Hillocks Jr., *Research on Written Composition*, pp. 248–249.

From his years of growing up in the area and living in Prairie View, Mr. Gomez knew that many of his students were great storytellers. They could come to class and tell detailed, funny, and metaphoric tales of encounters with truculent cows; or tell fluid, riveting tales about twisters, droughts, and other climatic conditions that helped to form the character of the prairie's inhabitants. What he found particularly frustrating was that even with this great narrative ability, they found *reading* stories to be a chore; they seemed to have little sense of the relationship between the stories they told so easily and those provided by their textbooks. Furthermore, the stories that many of his students told took full advantage of the colloquial dialect they spoke, using it for exaggeration, humor, and other effects, at times echoing the techniques of the frontier narratives of Pecos Bill, Paul Bunyan, and other legendary figures of the American West, as well as the great storytellers of the Native American and Mexican American communities.

I suggest that students must be *taught* the codes needed to participate fully in the mainstream of American life, not by being forced to attend to hollow, inane, decontextualized sub-skills, but rather within the context of meaningful communicative endeavors; that they must be allowed the resource of the teacher's expert knowledge, while being helped to acknowledge their own "expertness" as well; and that even while students are assisted in learning the culture of power, they must also be helped to learn about the arbitrariness of those codes and about the power relationships they represent.

Lisa Delpit, *Other People's Children*, p. 45.

Mr. Gomez thought he could take advantage of his students' narrative knowledge in the classroom by using it as a foundation for their study of language usage and for their understanding of literary stories. He decided to develop a unit in storytelling that would both establish story scripts for reading literature and reveal the appropriateness of different language codes for different communicative situations. In Mr. Gomez's view, the storytelling unit would help create equity in classes in which students arrived with a wide variety of knowledge, skill, and preparedness. By focusing on storytelling he could provide all students with equal opportunities to contribute to the class and have subject-matter expertise. Regardless of their other academic performances, all had abundant material to draw on for storytelling, and all were well versed in the narrative styles of their communities. The unit would also allow them to use their rural dialect in productive, acceptable ways, and help them see the relationship between their own narrative techniques and those of published storytellers. Ultimately, Mr. Gomez would help them use their stories as a bridge to both story structure and language usage. In addition the unit could provide integration with two other areas of the curriculum: He could incorporate it into a literature unit on Greek mythology that centered on narratives, and could also relate it to a social studies unit on ancient history taught by one of his colleagues at about the same point in the semester.

Mr. Gomez wanted to broaden students' understanding of the ways in which narratives are created and how they are understood by readers. To do so he supplemented the literature anthology's Greek myths with myths from the three primary cultures of his students: Anglo-Western, Mexican, and Native American. These additional literary works, he felt, would increase student interest in the Greek mythology from their anthology and help illuminate aspects of storytelling that could help them improve their own writing. Among his goals in connecting students' personal narratives to Greek mythology was to help relate students' cultural knowledge to literature written in a remote time and place by revealing the functions of storytelling regardless of the story's origins.

I argue that the narratives of Chicano men and women are predominantly critical and ideological. This does not mean that they simply represent a given set of doctrines or dogmas. Rather, it means that as oppositional ideological forms Chicano narratives signify the imaginary ways in which historical men and women live out their lives in a class society, and how the values, concepts, and ideas purveyed by the mainstream, hegemonic American culture that tie them to their social functions seek to prevent them from attaining a true knowledge of society as a whole. My study shows how Chicano narratives, individually as texts and together as a genre, confront and circumscribe the limiting ideologies imposed upon them (and sometimes created from within Mexican American culture itself) and how they have in complex ways determined the horizons within which their history has emerged.

Ramón Saldívar, *Chicano Narrative*, p. 6.

Mr. Gomez decided to start by having students tell their own stories orally. He asked for volunteers to tell tales based on their work experiences. Several of the class's more renowned tale spinners gladly took the opportunity to entertain their classmates. He encouraged students to enjoy the stories but also cautioned them that they should be prepared to discuss what they were about and what narrative devices they relied on.

Students apply a wide range of strategies to comprehend, interpret, evaluate, and appreciate texts. They draw on their prior experience, their interactions with other readers and writers, their knowledge of word meaning and other texts, their word identification strategies, and their understanding of textual features (e.g., sound-letter correspondence, sentence structure, context, graphics).

One of our major concerns was that many of the stories [Arapaho] children wrote didn't seem to "go anywhere." The stories just ambled along with no definite start or finish, no climaxes or conclusions. I decided to ask Pius Moss [the school elder] about these stories, since he is a master Arapaho storyteller himself. I learned about a distinctive difference between Arapaho stories and stories I was accustomed to hearing, reading, and telling. Pius Moss explained that Arapaho stories are not written down, they're told in what we might call serial form, continued night after night. A "good" story is one that lasts seven nights. . . .

When I asked Pius Moss why Arapaho stories never seem to have an "ending," he answered that there is no ending to life, and stories are about Arapaho life, so there is no need for a conclusion. My colleagues and I talked about what Pius had said, and we decided that we would encourage our students to choose whichever type of story they wished to write: we would try to listen and read in appropriate ways.

Gail Martin, *Reclaiming the Classroom*, pp. 166–167.

After several tales were related, Mr. Gomez had the students work in small groups to analyze the features of the different narratives they had heard. In the follow-up class discussion, some students said that some stories sounded more "right" to their ears than others. For instance, Janice, a Native American student, had told the following story:

On our ranch we eat wild honey. To find the hive we start by finding the bees wherever they get their water, like at a little pond where the cows water. The bees that make honey are real smart. When they leave the water to go back to the hive, they go in different directions. You have to know bees in order to follow them back to the hive. They fly high so you can barely see them, so you have to have good eyesight and see them as they cross the sunbeams. Once you spot the bees, you follow them as they fly lower and lower to the ground. The lower they get, the closer to the hive they are. If you get to the hive and the honey isn't ready, you leave it and come back another time.

Other kinds of bees are easier to follow. They fly lower, and the ones who fly the fastest are carrying water back to a hollow tree where they make a honeycomb. They are the ones you follow. You have to smoke the hive to get the honeycomb. You do that by building a fire just underneath the hollow and waving the smoke in. These bees are hard to smoke out, and you usually get stung when you get the honey.

Some kinds of bees also get smoked, but don't fight as hard, in fact they want to protect the queen bee so they just take off when you smoke them. These are the kinds of bees you use when you grow your own honey instead of getting it wild. They're fun to watch. They use mesquite gum and cottonwood mulch and make a ball for their hive. They start doing this in the spring.

Willie, one of the boys in the class, commented that this story just didn't seem like a story to him: "Nothin' happened," he said. "She just talked about getting honey. That ain't no story, that's just about bees."

Janice said, "What do you mean it's not a story? I told what happens when you get honey. That's a story."

"Yeah," said Willie, "you told about getting honey, but I mean, there was no plot, you know, nothin' happened. Story's got to have some action."

"Maybe for you, but not for me," said Janice.

Land is people. We have come far from this correlation, but return is not impossible. In many Native American languages the words "people" and "land" are indistinguishable and inseparable. . . . These are the kinds of relationships we must never forget. Our land is our strength, our people the land, one and the same, as it always has been and always will be. Remembering is all.

Geary Hobson, *The Remembered Earth*, p. 11.

The class discussed this point further, with some students agreeing with Willie that stories needed to have a clear story line and climax, and others feeling that stories like Janice's stood as narratives. The class did not reach consensus on story structure, but their discussion raised a number of issues that provided the basis for their subsequent reading of Greek myths. Mr. Gomez, for instance, asked students why they told stories and students offered a variety of reasons: to entertain people, to share their experiences with others, to get other people's attention, to give their point of view. He then asked, what do the subject matter and relationships of a story tell about the outlook of the storyteller? The students found that some students told stories in which they triumphed over some conflict and saw the storytellers as being strong, resourceful, boastful, competitive, and as possessing other dominant traits. Other stories were about relationships between friends and how they developed through some experience, which the students felt revealed that the storytellers were caring, friendly, supportive, and otherwise nurturing. Some stories had the sort of clear plot and action preferred by Willie; others, like Janice's, did not involve a definite course of action and resolution.

You will also find more attention given to the family; la familia and all the relationships involved therein are very important in Chicano literature. The relationship with the elders in a family provides a valuable learning context for our younger generation. The elders are the roots of our cultural ways. . . . The voice of the woman writer in these stories should draw special attention. Chicano culture is patriarchal in orientation, and as more and more Chicanas write they influence not only the content of the literature but also the culture itself. If literature is a liberating experience, then the voice of the Chicana writer in our culture is one of the most influential in helping to shape and change the cultural ways.

Rudolfo Anaya, foreword to *Growing Up Chicana/o*, p. 8.

After the class had discussed the variety of narrative features found in the students' stories, Mr. Gomez assigned a series of myths from the class anthology. He asked the students to focus on several issues in their reading and discussion of the Greek myths: How are these myths similar to and different from the ones told by students? What purposes did these myths serve for the ancient Greeks? What are the relationships between people and nature in these myths? How are men and women represented, especially in relation to one another? What is the story structure? Of what value are ancient Greek myths in the modern world? What do myths tell about the belief systems of the people who tell them?

To consider these questions, students returned to the same groups that they had worked in to analyze their narratives. One group consisted of three white students, Clint, Cody, and Dawn, and one Native American student, Pam. They looked at three Greek myths: King Midas, Phaeton and the chariot of the sun, and Daedalus and Icarus. Clint began their discussion of the myths:

Clint: Well, seems to me these myths are about some pretty stupid folks.

Dawn: How so?

Clint: Just look at 'em! Every one of 'em does something stupid and pretty near gets killed.

Cody: That one dude did get killed.

Pam: Icarus or whatever.

Cody: Yeah, both him and that other dude both tried to fly and lost control.

Pam: And the king lost control too when he wanted to turn everything to gold.

Dawn: They all got greedy and wanted stuff they couldn't have and ended up losing stuff.

Clint: So I guess Greek myths are about greedy folks who end up being losers, right?

Pam: Well, you sorta get like a little moral at the end, like don't worship gold, or don't disobey what your parents say or nothin' like that.

Cody: Yeah, two are about kids who disobey their fathers and fly out of control, and one's about a father who disobeys his daughter and can't even eat no more. And the moral thing says, "Don't be greedy no more."

— Students develop an understanding of and respect for diversity in language use, patterns, and dialects across cultures, ethnic groups, geographic regions, and social roles.

— Students use spoken, written, and visual language to accomplish their own purposes (e.g., for learning, enjoyment, persuasion, and the exchange of information).

— Students read a wide range of literature from many periods in many genres to build an understanding of the many dimensions (e.g., philosophical, ethical, aesthetic) of human experience.

Dawn: Mr. Gomez says we're supposed to compare these Greek myths to our own stories.

Clint: Well these are sure different from Cody's story. He was greedy, all right, but he didn't get no moralizin' about it.

Pam: That's cause he lied. He ain't half as much a hero as he made himself out to be in that story.

Cody: Bull! I don't need to tell no lies. I brung them calfs in before the twister hit and wasn't no greed about it. If I hadn't done it, they'd of died. Least you could tell what my story was about, unlike that story about bees, which wasn't even a story at all but just about how to find honey.

Pam: Sounded like a story to me. What was wrong with it?

Cody: Didn't have no ending, and nothin' happened anyhow, just how to get honey, I mean, what kind of story is that?

Pam: Sounded like a story to me.

The students had difficulty resolving their differences about whether Janice's description of bees constituted a story or not, and about what a narrative entails. Their effort to consider the Greek myths in terms of their own narratives raised many of the same issues they'd discussed when analyzing the features of student stories.

Students apply knowledge of language structure, language conventions (e.g., spelling and punctuation), media techniques, figurative language, and genre to create, critique, and discuss print and nonprint texts.

[T]he primary assumptions tribespeople make can be seen as static only in that these people acknowledge the essential harmony of all things and see all things as being of equal value in the scheme of things, denying the opposition, dualism, and isolation (separateness) that characterize non-Indian thought. . . . [T]he non-Christian tribal person assumes a place in creation that is dynamic, creative, and responsive. Further, tribal people allow all animals, vegetables, and minerals (the entire biota, in short) the same or even greater privileges. . . . Another difference between these two ways of perceiving reality lies in the tendency of the American Indian to view space as spherical and time as cyclical, whereas the non-Indian tends to view space as linear and time as sequential. The circular concept requires all "points" that make up the sphere of being to have a significant identity and function, while the linear model assumes that some "points" are more significant than others. . . . Because of the basic assumption of the wholeness or unity of the universe, our natural and necessary relationship to all life is evident; all phenomena we witness within or "outside" ourselves are, like us, intelligent manifestations of the intelligent universe from which they arise, as do all things of earth and the cosmos beyond.

Paula Gunn Allen, *Studies in American Indian Literature*, pp. 5–9.

Students develop an understanding of and respect for diversity in language use, patterns, and dialects across cultures, ethnic groups, geographic regions, and social roles.

Students adjust their use of spoken, written, and visual language (e.g., conventions, style, vocabulary) to communicate effectively with a variety of audiences and for different purposes.

In addition to helping students consider the different structures narration can take, the analysis of narratives also turned to language usage. The class discussions and small-group conversations engaged students in an examination of the appropriateness of particular language structures in different situations. During one class discussion Mr. Gomez asked students if one style of speech, such as the ungrammatical language that was characteristic of frontier myths, would be appropriate for telling a Greek myth. This question led to a consideration of the sufficiency of any single dialect for all social situations:

Patsy: I talk more proper in school than I do at home, but not much.

Vince: Mostly around town I talk the same; don't matter if I'm at home or in the barn or at the barbershop, folks around here talk the same mostly.

Dolly: Yeah, don't matter to you 'cause you don't never go nowhere else. If I go to the city I don't want to sound country, so I got to learn to talk more proper.

Alan: Yeah, but if some city boy come out here and tried to sell my dad some feed by talkin' all proper, he'd never sell a grain cause my dad don't trust people who talk like that.

Reba: That's right, we got our own way of talkin' proper down here, and that's the way I talk.

Mr. Gomez: Have you ever wondered what would happen if you grew up and could only talk country?

Reba: That's what I am, so that's the way I talk, thank you very much.

Vince: But if you ever change your mind and want to, you know, go to college or go work in an office in the city, you can't go 'round sayin', "I'm fixin' t' merge with your company, ain't nothin' t' argue with." You gotta know how to speak their language.

Clint: But country works for country folk. Can you imagine tunin' in to the country and western station and listening to songs in proper English? Nobody'd buy them. Country singers gotta sing in the country way of talkin'.

Mr. Gomez: Clint, you've got an interesting point there. How about if you bring in some of your music and we'll try to rewrite the lyrics in proper English, and see how it sounds?

Students conduct research on issues and interests by generating ideas and questions, and by posing problems. They gather, evaluate, and synthesize data from a variety of sources (e.g., print and nonprint texts, artifacts, people) to communicate their discoveries in ways that suit their purpose and audience.

The next day Clint and other students brought in cassettes of country and western performers and played songs in which the singers routinely violated the rules of their grammar textbook. Students then worked to rewrite the songs in proper English to see how they would work as country and western songs. Some students brought in guitars and actually performed the revised lyrics to satiric effect. They agreed that the performers could not make a living singing country and western music that used standard English; it just didn't sound country.

Following this practice in translating lyrics from one dialect to another, Mr. Gomez asked students to retell a myth from one culture in the style of another. To do so they needed to understand the syntax, vocabulary, narrative structure, people/nature relationships, male/female roles, and other traits of both mythic traditions they considered. Mr. Gomez encouraged students to work in small groups to discuss possibilities, and eventually some of the students worked in pairs to collaborate on their myths. Students needed to make decisions about which traditions and which specific myths to focus on and needed to conduct a final, detailed study of the traditions they were working with. Some students decided to tell a Greek myth using the tradition of the American West: Prometheus became Pecosius, hogtying the vulture who came to eat his liver and putting him to the test of fire. Other students turned the tables in other directions, taking Western stories and retelling them in standard diction using other narrative structures and value systems. Cody and Clint collaborated to rewrite the story of Daedalus and Icarus as a tale of the West:

The Myth of Deadwood and Ickypuss

Well folks, let me tell ya'll about a couple of good old boys named Deadwood and Ickypuss. Deadwood was Ickypuss's daddy. They'd been captured by some bad dudes and was put in a shed on an island in the middle of a mighty big lake. All they could do was set there and watch them birds fly, just wishin' they had guns so they could do some shootin'.

Well, after a while things got mighty borin', and they wished they could hightail it out of there. They finally busted out of the shed but still were stuck on that island and couldn't do nothin' about it.

Ickypuss didn't mind watchin' the birds fly all day, and amused hisself by throwin' rocks at them. But sittin' on that island day after day made Deadwood more ornerier'n a long-tailed cat in a room full of rockin' chairs, and so he started fixin' to bust loose. One day Ickypuss actually hit one of them birds and killed it, and he brought it to his daddy to show it off. Ickypuss said, "If I had me some wings I'd just fly on out of here." His daddy thought real quick'n grabbed that bird, plucked off its feathers and told Ickypuss to go kill some more.

When they had more feathers than you could shake a stick at Deadwood melted some wax and made two big ol' wings and stuck them on his arms. They worked real good, so he made another pair and put them on ol' Ickypuss's arms. Those two boys whooped it up, flappin' around and soon they was flyin' off into the sky.

Well ol' Ickypuss got kinda carried away and started flyin' way off into the clouds. Next thing you know he was gettin' mighty close to the sun, and fairly soon his wings started to meltin' and he started to droppin' back to earth. Deadwood saw what was happenin' and he'd have none of it. He swooped on up and flapped his wings so hard the sun went out. He then flew down and caught Ickypuss on his back and flew back down to earth, which was mighty cold by that time. But that didn't matter none, Deadwood just called it night and then took himself a well-deserved nap.

Students had the opportunity to read their stories to their classmates and enjoy one another's translations.

To conclude the storytelling unit, Mr. Gomez asked the students to work in small groups to prepare a set of guides to "How to Talk in Prairie View." Students identified local expressions and provided a pronunciation key, origins, definitions, and examples of usage. When each group was finished, they compiled the contributions into a comprehensive guide. Mr. Gomez then reached an agreement with the local weekly newspaper to have the guide published in the "School Report" section, with each contributing student's name listed as co-author.

[T]he community is not . . . a structure of institutions capable of objective definition and description. Instead, we try to understand "community" by seeking to capture members' experience of it. Instead of asking, "what does it look like to us? What are its theoretical implications?", we ask, "What does it appear to mean to its members?" Rather than describing analytically the form of the structure from an external vantage point, we are attempting to penetrate the structure, to look *outwards* from its core.

Anthony P. Cohen, *The Symbolic Construction of Community*, pp. 19–20.

Mr. Gomez was able to follow through on this unit in his subsequent instruction. The students began to pay attention to the speakers' diction in the literature they read, discussing how a person's speech can indicate the time period he or she lives in, the region of the country, the expectations of the people in the surrounding society, and other related factors. Their attention to language codes then returned to their own speech, and the class considered such questions as: What are the characteristics of the speech used by people in Prairie View? With whom is it effective and proper to use this speech? What type of people will form negative opinions of people who use this speech? What will their impressions be? Is their opinion important? What are the consequences of learning to speak in only one way? What variations on English are available to residents of Prairie View, and what is the result of both learning them and not learning them?

Many students who never intended to leave Prairie View were, like Reba, adamant about the quality of their own speech and resentful of people who put on airs about how properly they spoke. Others felt they needed to learn to speak in more than one dialect in order to be successful in society. In general, the discussion about language propriety provided a context for the inevitable preparation for the standardized state language exam, which Mr. Gomez was required to devote class time to each spring.

Overall Eddie Gomez was happy with the unit on storytelling. He had brought issues of language usage to students' attention without subjecting them to what he felt was the oppressive and ineffective methodology of the grammar textbook. Although they had not practiced the kinds of grammar problems found on the state-mandated standardized tests, they had used language in ways that addressed their communication needs and considered the economic consequences of following different speech conventions.

He was also pleased that he had been able to connect his own students' cultural knowledge of storytelling with the required unit on mythology from the literature anthology. Students had responded with greater interest than they had in the past when he had approached Greek myths as a separate, remote genre. By helping students to see the mythology of their own prairie culture, he was able to help them see some purpose in the myths of ancient times.

— Students apply knowledge of language structure, language conventions (e.g., spelling and punctuation), media techniques, figurative language, and genre to create, critique, and discuss print and nonprint texts.

Standards in Practice

Mr. Gomez's unit on myth and narration enables students to consider their own cultural heritages, and the ways in which those heritages are manifested in the stories of their communities, as important texts in their school experiences. Their experiences with community-based narratives provide the basis for their reading of classic myths from a variety of cultures. Critical to their understanding of different narrative conventions is their consideration of appropriate vocabulary, grammar, syntax, diction, and story structure, and their willingness to accept the validity of narrative approaches different from those they are familiar with. Their production of their own myths requires them to consider the appropriateness of different conventions, and to engage in an extended process of composition to develop finished narratives. The issue of dialect is critical to the activity of students in this class, with an understanding of the communicative functions of specific sets of conventions crucial to their determination of how to speak under different sets of circumstances. Such an understanding is important to their ability to participate fruitfully in a variety of literacy communities, and to use language to accomplish their own purposes.

Resources

Rural Education

Books

Benally, E. R. (1987). *Issues in American Indian education, Mexican American education, migrant education, outdoor education, rural education, and small schools.* Las Cruces, NM: ERIC Clearinghouse on Rural Education and Small Schools.

Dillman, D. A., & Hobbs, D. J. (Eds.). (1982). *Rural society in the U.S.: Issues for the 1980s.* Boulder, CO: Westview Press.

Hobbs, D. J. (1987). *Learning to find the "niches": Rural education and vitalizing rural communities.* Elmhurst, IL: North Central Regional Educational Laboratory.

McPherson, G. H. (1972). *Small town teacher.* Cambridge, MA: Harvard University Press.

Nachtigal, P. M. (1980). *Improving rural schools.* Washington, D.C.: National Institute of Education.

Nachtigal, P. M. (Ed.). (1982). *Rural education: In search of a better way.* Boulder, CO: Westview Press.

Peshkin, A. (1978). *Growing up American: Schooling and the survival of community.* Chicago: University of Chicago Press.

Sher, J. P. (Ed.). (1977). *Education in rural America: A reassessment of conventional wisdom.* Boulder, CO: Westview Press.

Sher, J. P. (Ed.). (1981). *Rural education in urbanized nations: Issues and innovations.* Boulder, CO: Westview Press.

Sherwood, T. (1989). *Nontraditional education in rural districts.* Charleston, WV: ERIC Clearinghouse on Rural Education and Small Schools.

Stillman, P. (1995). *Planting by the moon: On life in a mountain hamlet.* Portsmouth, NH: Heinemann.

White, S. J. (1981). *Exemplary rural education and economic development initiatives: State-of-the-art report.* Washington, D.C.: The Institute.

Journals

Bulletin of the Department of Rural Education, the National Education Association of the United States, Department of Rural Education

Journal of Research in Rural Education, College of Education, University of Maine

Research in Rural Education, College of Education, University of Maine

Yearbook of the National Education Association of the United States, Department of Rural Education

Organizations and Committees

National Rural Education Association (Fort Collins, CO)

NCTE Assembly on the Literature and Culture of Appalachia

NCTE Assembly of Rural Teachers of English

NCTE Commission on Rural Schools (subcommittee of the Conference on English Leadership)

NCTE Commission on Teacher Education for Teachers of Urban, Rural, and Suburban Students of Color (subcommittee of the Conference on English Education)

Teaching Grammar and Dialect

Books

Allen, H., & Linn, M. D. (Eds.). (1986). *Dialect and language variation.* Orlando, FL: Academic Press.

Andrews, L. (1993). *Language exploration and awareness: A resource book for teachers.* White Plains, NY: Longman.

Baron, D. (1989). *Declining grammar and other essays on the English vocabulary.* Urbana, IL: National Council of Teachers of English.

Baron, D. (1994). *Guide to home language repair.* Urbana, IL: National Council of Teachers of English.

Bean, W., & Bouffler, C. (1987). *Spell by writing.* Rozelle NSW, Australia: Primary English Teaching Association.

Belanoff, P., Rorschach, B., Rakijas, M., & Millis, C. (1993). *The right handbook: Grammar and usage in context* (2nd ed.). Portsmouth, NH: Boynton/Cook Publishers.

Cazden, C. B. (1988). *Classroom discourse: The language of teaching and learning.* Portsmouth, NH: Heinemann.

Cazden, C. B., John, V. P., & Hymes, D. (Eds.). (1972). *Functions of language in the classroom.* New York: Teachers College Press.

Clark, V. P., Eschholz, P. A., & Rosan, A. F. (Eds.). (1985). *Language: Introductory readings* (4th ed.). New York: St. Martin's Press.

Farr, M., & Daniels, H. (1986). *Language diversity and writing instruction.* Urbana, IL: ERIC Clearinghouse on Reading and Communication Skills.

Gee, J. (1990). *Social linguistics and literacies: Ideology in discourses.* New York: Falmer Press.

Gilyard, K. (1991). *Voices of the self: A study of language competence.* Detroit: Wayne State University Press.

Heath, S. B. (1983). *Ways with words: Language, life, and work in communities and classrooms.* New York: Cambridge University Press.

Hillocks, G., Jr. (1986). *Research on written composition: New directions for teaching.* Urbana, IL: ERIC Clearinghouse on Reading and Communication Skills and National Conference on Research in English.

Hodges, R. E. (1982). *Improving spelling and vocabulary in the secondary school.* Urbana, IL: ERIC Clearinghouse on Reading and Communication Skills and National Council of Teachers of English.

Hunter, S., & Wallace, R. (Eds.). (1995). *The place of grammar in writing instruction: Past, present, future.* Portsmouth, NH: Boynton/Cook Publishers.

Hymes, D. (1974). *Foundations in sociolinguistics: An ethnographic approach.* Philadelphia, PA: University of Pennsylvania Press.

Labov, W. (1972). *Sociolinguistic patterns.* Philadelphia, PA: University of Pennsylvania Press.

Morenberg, M. (1991). *Doing grammar.* New York: Oxford University Press.

Noguchi, R. R. (1991). *Grammar and the teaching of writing: Limits and possibilities.* Urbana, IL: National Council of Teachers of English.

Philips, S. (1982). *The invisible culture: Communication in the classroom and community on the Warm Springs Indian Reservation.* New York, NY: Longman.

Rose, M. (1989). *Lives on the boundary: The struggles of America's underprepared.* New York: Free Press.

Shaughnessy, M. P. (1977). *Errors and expectations: A guide for the teacher of basic writing.* New York: Oxford University Press.

Shuy, R. W. (1967). *Discovering American dialects.* Urbana, IL: National Council of Teachers of English.

Strong, W. (1986). *Creative approaches to sentence combining.* Urbana, IL: ERIC Clearinghouse on Reading and Communication Skills and National Council of Teachers of English.

Weaver, C. (1979). *Grammar for teachers: Perspectives and definitions.* Urbana, IL: National Council of Teachers of English.

Willinsky, J. (1988). *The well-tempered tongue: The politics of standard English in the high school.* New York: Teachers College Press.

Wolfram, W. (1991). *Dialects and American English.* Englewood Cliffs, NJ: Prentice-Hall.

Organizations and Committees

American Dialect Society
National Council of Teachers of Grammar
NCTE Assembly for the Teaching of English Grammar
NCTE Commission on Language

World Wide Web Site

This is the address of the American Dialect Society.
http://www.msstate.edu/Archives/ADS

Anglo-Western Tales

Books

Botkin, B. A. (1951). *A treasury of western folklore.* New York: Crown Publishers.

Botkin, B. A. (Ed.). (1990). *A treasury of western folklore.* New York: Bonanza Books.

Cunningham, K. (Ed.). (1990). *The oral tradition of the American West: Adventure, courtship, family, and place in traditional recitation.* Little Rock, AR: August House.

Dary, D. (1989). *Cowboy culture: A saga of five centuries.* Lawrence: University Press of Kansas.

Garry, J. (1994). *The first liar never has a chance: Curley, Jack, Bill, & other characters of the hills, brush, & plains.* New York: Crown Publishers.

Greenway, J. (Ed.). (1969). *Folklore of the great West: Selections from eighty-three years of the Journal of American Folklore.* Palo Alto, CA: American West Publishing Co.

Milner, C. A., O'Connor, C. A., & Sandweiss, M. A. (Eds.). (1994). *Oxford history of the American West.* New York: Oxford University Press.

San Souci, R. D., & Pinkney, J. (Eds.). (1993). *Cut from the same cloth: American women of myth, legend, and tall tales.* New York: Philomel Books.

Virgines, G. E. (1984). *Western legends and lore.* Wauwatosa, WI: Leather Stocking Books.

Journals

Journal of American Folklore, American Folklore Society

Southern Folklore Quarterly, University Press of Kentucky

Native American Tales

Books

Allen, P. G. (Ed.). (1983). *Studies in American Indian literature: Critical essays and course designs.* New York: Modern Language Association.

Allen, P. G. (1986). *The sacred hoop: Recovering the feminine in American Indian traditions.* Boston: Beacon Press.

Allen, P. G. (Ed.). (1989). *Spider Woman's granddaughters: Traditional tales and contemporary writing by Native American women.* Boston: Beacon Press.

Allen, P. G. (Ed.). (1994). *Voice of the turtle: American Indian literature.* New York: Ballantine Books.

Armstrong, J. (Ed.). (1993). *Looking at the words of our people: First nation's analysis of literature.* Penticton, British Columbia: Theytus Books.

Bataille, G. M., & Sands, K. M. (1984). *American Indian women telling their lives.* Lincoln, NE: University of Nebraska Press.

Beck, M. L. (1989). *Heroes and heroines of Tlingit-Haida legend.* Anchorage, AK: Northwest Books.

Bierhorst, J. (1985). *The mythology of North America.* New York: Morrow.

Bruchac, J. (Ed.). (1994). *Returning the gift: Poetry and prose from the First North American Native Writers' Festival.* Tucson, AZ: University of Arizona Press.

Bruchac, J., & Ross, G. (1994). *The girl who married the moon: Tales from Native North America.* New York: Bridgewater Books.

Caduto, M. J., & Bruchac, J. (1988). *Keepers of the earth: Native American stories and environmental activities for children.* Golden, CO: Fulcrum.

Day, A. G. (1951). *The sky clears: Poetry of the American Indians.* New York: Macmillan.

Erdoes, R., & Ortiz, A. (Eds.). (1984). *American Indian myths and legends.* New York: Pantheon Books.

Harjo, J. (1989). *Secrets from the center of the world.* Tucson, AZ: Sun Tracks (Vol. 17) and University of Arizona Press.

Hobson, G. (Ed.). (1980). *The remembered earth: An anthology of contemporary Native American literature.* Albuquerque, NM: University of New Mexico Press.

Katz, J. B. (Ed.). (1977). *I am the fire of time: The voices of Native American women.* New York: Dutton.

Ramsey, J. (Ed.). (1977). *Coyote was going there: Indian literature of the Oregon country.* Seattle: University of Washington Press.

Sarris, G. (1993). *Keeping slug woman alive: A holistic approach to American Indian texts.* Berkeley, CA: University of California Press.

Sarris, G. (Ed.). (1994). *The sound of rattles and clappers: A collection of new California Indian writing.* Tucson, AZ: University of Arizona Press.

Stensland, A. L. (1979). *Literature by and about the American Indian: An annotated bibliography.* Urbana, IL: National Council of Teachers of English.

Turner, F. W. III. (Ed.). (1977). *The portable North American Indian reader.* New York: Penguin.

Vecsey, C. (1988). *Imagine ourselves richly: Mythic narratives of North American Indians.* New York: Crossroad.

Velie, A. R. (Ed.). (1979). *American Indian literature: An anthology.* Norman, OK: University of Oklahoma Press.

Journals

American Indian Culture and Research Journal, American Indian Studies Center, UCLA

American Indian Quarterly, Native American Studies, University of California–Berkeley

Journal of Cherokee Studies, Cherokee Museum, Cherokee, NC

Studies in American Indian Literature, Association for Studies in American Indian Literatures

World Wide Web Site

http://ukanaix.cc.ukans.edu/marc/native_main.html

Mexican American Tales

Books

de Dwyer, C. C. (Ed.). (1975). *Chicano voices.* Boston: Houghton Mifflin.

Duran, D. F. (1979). *Latino materials: A multimedia guide for children and young adults.* New York: N. Schuman.

Kurtycz, M., & Kobeh, A. G. (1984). *Tigers and opossums: Animal legends.* Boston: Little, Brown.

López, T. A. (Ed.). (1993). *Growing up Chicana/o: An anthology.* New York: William Morrow and Co.

Martinez, J. A., & Lomeli, F. A. (Eds.). (1985). *Chicano literature: A reader's encyclopedia.* Westport, CT: Greenwood Press.

Paredes, A. (Ed.). (1970). *Folktales of Mexico.* Chicago: University of Chicago Press.

Paredes, A. (1976). *A Texas-Mexican "Cancionero": Folksongs of the lower border.* Urbana, IL: University of Illinois Press.

Peña, M. (1985). *The Texas-Mexican conjunto: History of a working class music.* Austin, TX: University of Texas Press.

Rocard, M. (1989). *The children of the sun: Mexican-Americans in the literature of the United States* (E. G. Brown, Jr., Trans.). Tucson, AZ: University of Arizona Press.

Saldívar, R. (1990). *Chicano narrative: The dialectics of difference.* Madison, WI: University of Wisconsin Press.

Tatum, C. M. (1982). *Chicano literature.* Boston: Twayne Publishers.

World Wide Web Site

http://latino.sscnet.ucla.edu/women/womenHP.html

World Mythology

Books

Ann, M. (1993). *Goddesses in world mythology.* Santa Barbara, CA: ABC-CLIO.

Bulfinch, T. (1968). *Bulfinch's mythology.* London: Spring Books.

Cotterell, A. (1989). *The Macmillan illustrated encyclopedia of myths & legends.* New York: Macmillan.

Kohn, R. T. (1985). *Mythology for young people: A reference guide.* New York: Garland.

Larrington, C. (Ed.). (1992). *The feminist companion to mythology.* London: Pandora.

Maranda, P. (Ed.). (1972). *Mythology: Selected readings.* Baltimore: Penguin Books.

Mercatante, A. S. (1988). *The Facts on File encyclopedia of world mythology and legend.* New York: Facts on File.

Randazzo, S. (1993). *Mythmaking on Madison Avenue: How advertisers apply the power of myth & symbolism to create leadership brands.* Chicago: Probus Publishing Company.

Robinson, H. S. (1961). *Myths and legends of all nations.* New York: Bantam Books.

Shinn, T. J. (1986). *Worlds within women: Myth and mythmaking in fantastic literature by women.* New York: Greenwood Press.

Journal

Parabola, Society for the Study of Myth and Tradition

Situated Learning

Books, Chapters, and Articles

Bartholomae, D. (1985). Inventing the university. In M. Rose (Ed.), *When a writer can't write: Studies in writer's block and other composing process problems* (pp. 134–165). New York: Guilford.

Brown, J. S., Collins, A., & Duguid, P. (1989a). Situated cognition and the culture of learning. *Educational Researcher, 18*(1), 32–42.

Carter, M. (1990). The idea of expertise: An exploration of cognitive and social dimensions of writing. *College Composition and Communication, 41*(3), 265–286.

Cazden, C. B. (in press). Selective traditions: Readings of Vygotsky in writing pedagogy. In D. Hicks (Ed.), *Child discourse and social learning: An interdisciplinary perspective.* New York: Cambridge University Press.

Chaiklin, S., & Lave, J. (Eds.). (1993). *Understanding practice.* Cambridge: Cambridge University Press.

Collins, A., Brown, J. S., & Holum, A. (1991). Cognitive apprenticeship: Making things visible. *American Educator, 15*(3), 6–11, 38–46.

Colomb, G. (1988). *Disciplinary "secrets" and the apprentice writer: The lessons for critical thinking.* Upper Montclair, NJ: Montclair State College Institute for Critical Thinking.

Dyson, A. H. (1993). *Social worlds of children learning to write in an urban primary school.* New York: Teachers College Press.

Farr, M. (1993). Essayist literacy and other verbal performances. *Written Communication, 10*(1), 4–38.

Gilmore, P., & Glatthorn, A. (Eds.). (1982). *Children in and out of school: Ethnography and education.* Washington, D.C.: Center for Applied Linguistics.

Moll, L. C. (Ed.). (1990). *Vygotsky and education: Instructional implications and applications of sociohistorical psychology.* New York: Cambridge University Press.

Perkins, D. N., & Salomon, G. (1988). Teaching for transfer. *Educational Leadership, 46*(1), 22–32.

Perkins, D. N., & Salomon, G. (1989). Are cognitive skills context bound? *Educational Researcher, 18*(1), 16–25.

Rogoff, B. (1990). *Apprenticeship in thinking: Cognitive development in social context.* New York: Oxford University Press.

Rogoff, B., & Lave, J. (Eds.). (1984). *Everyday cognition: Its development in social context.* Cambridge, MA: Harvard University Press.

Smagorinsky, P., & Smith, M. W. (1992). The nature of knowledge in composition and literary understanding: The question of specificity. *Review of Educational Research, 62*(3), 279–305.

Vygotsky, L. S. (1978). *Mind in society: The development of higher psychological processes.* Cambridge: Harvard University Press.

Vygotsky, L. S. (1987). Thinking and speech. In L. S. Vygotsky, *Collected works* (Vol. 1, pp. 39–285). (R. Rieber & A. Carton, Eds.; N. Minick, Trans.). New York: Plenum.

Wells, G. (1987). *The meaning makers: Children learning language and using language to learn.* London: Hodder and Stoughton Educational.

Wertsch, J. V. (Ed.). (1985). *Culture, communication, and cognition: Vygotskian perspectives.* New York: Cambridge University Press.

Wertsch, J. V. (1991). *Voices of the mind: A sociocultural approach to mediated action.* Cambridge, MA: Harvard University Press.

Journals

Journal of Language and Social Psychology, Sage Publications

Mind, Culture, and Activity, Laboratory of Comparative Human Cognition, University of California at San Diego

E-mail Network

xmca@ucsd.edu

Publication of Student Writing

Journal

Merlyn's Pen, East Greenwich, RI

Organizations and Committees

NCTE Assembly for Advisors of Student Publications/Journalism Education Association

NCTE Committee on Promising Young Writers State Coordinators

NCTE Promising Young Writers Advisory Committee

NCTE Recognize Excellence in Student Literary Magazines Advisory Committee

NCTE State Leaders for Committee to Recognize Excellence in Student Literary Magazines

CHAPTER FOUR

THE COLOR OF THE CURRICULUM

Fair Oaks was a suburb of a Southeastern city. While not an exclusively wealthy community, it was a town whose most modest neighborhoods were neat, clean, and comfortably middle class. It was both a commuter town for the city in whose radius it rested and an established community in its own right, with its own historical society, cultural attractions, and office complexes. Residents of the town were mostly white, with about 15% of the townspeople Asian and 10% African American. Students tended to come from college-educated families and aspire to live the upper-middle-class life of their origins. Typically, 80% of each graduating class went on to college and a high percentage of those students earned college degrees.

Fair Oaks High School was a four-year public school serving about 2,000 students. There were twenty-two English teachers plus a set of volunteer aides (usually parents from the community) who assisted with grading papers, supervising collaborative group work, and other classroom responsibilities. Fifteen of the English teachers were women, seven were men, and all were white; according to the district personnel director, few minority candidates had ever applied for positions at Fair Oaks High School. The average level of seniority for the English department was seventeen years of service. Although some teachers came in with experience from other districts, teachers tended to stay at Fair Oaks once they were hired because of the high salaries, benefits, and favorable teaching conditions. Eighteen of the twenty-two English teachers had master's degrees, two held doctorates, and two were relatively recent hires in their twenties who had begun working on their master's degrees since joining the faculty.

Classes were tracked according to students' perceived ability and performance based on standardized test scores and recommendations from guidance counselors and teachers. Parents, however, could request a different placement than recommended by the school. There were three tracks: basic, regular, and honors. Most students in the top two tracks went on to college.

The English curriculum reflected the traditional values of the community. The department acquired an anthology series from a commercial publisher and built their curricular scope and sequence chart around the textbook's organization. Supplementary literature came from the familiar canon: *The Catcher in the Rye, A Separate Peace,* and *Ordinary People* in the sophomore year; *The Scarlet Letter, Huckleberry Finn,* and similar classics for juniors; *Beowulf, Hamlet, Pride and Prejudice,* and other standards of British literature for seniors preparing for college. Grammar instruction was featured during all four years of high school, with the focus on instruction derived from the grammar and composition textbook the district required. This textbook served as the source of much writing instruction as well, with the freshman year devoted to learning the basics of sentences and paragraphs, and the five-paragraph theme an emphasis of the sophomore through senior years.

Debbie Green was one of the two newly hired teachers in the English department. Like any faculty newcomer, she was given a teaching assignment that consisted of courses that remained after her more senior colleagues selected the classes they wanted to teach. Honors, AP classes, and the more rigorous senior electives (college composition, humanities, and British literature) typically went to the most senior faculty members, often becoming their bailiwicks for a decade and more. New faculty often taught several "basic" classes and one or two regular-track courses until someone retired. Ms. Green had taught the same assignment for all four of her years in the district: two sections of basic-track freshmen, one section of basic-track sophomores, and two sections of regular-track juniors. This year, a more senior colleague had gotten sick just before the beginning of school and Debbie Green had been asked to teach her senior year humanities course instead of the basic sophomore course.

The implied goal of the regular-track curriculum was to prepare students for college. As a result, the district administrators and parents expected teachers to provide relatively uniform instruction so that they all graduated with similar preparation. Teachers were expected to teach the same materials at roughly the same pace so that students who entered the sophomore year would all have had similar preparation in their freshman years, and so on throughout their four-year sequence of high school education.

Because most students at Fair Oaks High School succeeded in college, the faculty members as a whole were satisfied with the fundamental values of the curriculum. These values had changed little, and the most senior faculty members took pride in the stability of the school's traditions and the faculty's wisdom in sustaining them. Because the school always achieved an elite position in the annual rankings of schools provided by the metropolitan area newspaper, few had ever questioned the appropriateness of the school's mission or processes in pursuing it. The curriculum offered a stable canon of literature for students to read, one that graduates had said prepared them well for their first-year literature courses in college.

While Ms. Green agreed that the curriculum served many students very well, she felt troubled by the exclusive worldview that it offered. In many ways the literature reflected the life histories of the primarily white, middle-class student body she taught; even the more contemporary young adult literature of the sophomore year focused on white, middle-class students, mostly males, from suburbs and prep schools. On the one hand this emphasis was fine since many students seemed to find that the trials of the literary characters they encountered informed their own life experiences.

On the other hand, something was amiss. Slightly over half of her students were girls, yet relatively little of the literature in the curriculum was written by women or featured female protagonists. Furthermore, her minority students saw little of themselves in the curriculum. There were few Asian authors in the whole 9–12 scope and sequence, and the African American authors were primarily confined to the "Harlem Renaissance" unit in the junior anthology, a unit that a number of teachers either never got to or skipped over in their chronological approach to American literature. Ms. Green felt that the monochromatic, single-sex perspective of the literature not only ignored the experiences of her women and minority students, it provided the white males in her classes with narrow views that did not challenge them to see the world from a different perspective.

As Debbie Green's discomfort with the established curriculum grew, she considered ways to make changes to broaden the perspective it offered. Her reading of Alice Walker's *The Color Purple* in a graduate course provided the opportunity she sought. She found it to be a remarkable literary achievement, one that provided a view of male/female relationships not available in the standard curriculum. It also presented a view of the rural South from an African American perspective, something most of her students had never been exposed to. At the end of the first semester's first marking period, Ms. Green raised the prospect of reading the novel with her students, saying that she had read the book, found it interesting, and wondered if they would like to read it. A number of them expressed an interest and none objected, so Ms. Green decided to try to read the book with her seniors in the spring. Doing so, however, required her to go through a labyrinth of procedures seemingly designed to thwart efforts to change the curriculum.

[T]he processes of self-reflection and self-definition are influenced more when a work challenges the assumptions that the reader brings to the text. The point is simply that ethnic literature offers promising possibilities for novice readers of that ethnicity. This point of view does not contradict the claim that exposing students to multi-ethnic literature expands students' understanding and perceptions of other groups. (I agree wholeheartedly with this claim.) However, it must be remembered that literature curricula of U.S. high schools, on the whole, are not multi-ethnic and that African American students in huge numbers (as well as other groups . . .) do not fare well in public education. Freire (1970) argues correctly when he says that the poor and unempowered are empowered through dialogue and reflective contemplation about their own experiences, both politically, culturally, and personally. Close readings of an ethnic group's literature offer such possibilities. Freire (1970) is right to call for a pedagogy of the oppressed.

Carol D. Lee, *Signifying as a Scaffold for Literary Interpretation,* p. 145.

She began by talking informally with her colleagues. Most were discouraging, if not downright opprobrious, when they learned of her plans. Some said that the lesbianism in the book should automatically disqualify it from consideration because it would cause an uproar among many members of the community. Others wondered why she would want to change a curriculum that was already working so well. She also learned that some colleagues had begun referring to her as a "politically correct" young zealot who was out to radicalize the curriculum and indoctrinate the students into her own set of feminist values. Some of her colleagues believed she wanted to replace the great classics of yore with modern literature of unproven and suspect merit. A few did not disapprove of her idea, but said that they would wait and see what happened before offering their support.

Ms. Green went ahead in spite of the opposition and difficulty she would create for herself, convinced that the novel was worth teaching. She wrote a lengthy proposal to add the novel to the approved list of texts for the junior year and submitted it through the sequence of committees that approved of changes in the curriculum: the English department advisory board, the school curriculum committee, and finally the district board of education. The proposal met with qualified and reluctant acceptance at each point. Each committee required her to appear personally and respond to rigorous questioning about her rationale, motives, teaching methods, and objectives. Finally, early in the second semester, Ms. Green was granted permission to include *The Color Purple* among the novels she taught in her senior humanities course.

She taught the novel in the spring. At about that time she was finishing her master's degree course work in an English education program and decided that for her thesis she would do a self-study of her teaching of *The Color Purple*. In so doing she hoped to understand the reasons behind the immense resistance to including the novel in the curriculum and to illuminate the processes her students went through in reading and responding to it. Her master's degree program included an emphasis on "action" research and put her in touch with a metropolitan teacher-research group that maintained a network of teachers in the area. Based on her conception of teacher-research from both her graduate program and her participation in the network, she envisioned a study that drew on three types of data: (1) she would maintain a journal reflecting intensely on the progress of the unit, (2) she would engage in oral inquiry by meeting with the metropolitan teacher-research group regularly to discuss her experiences and those of the other group members, and (3) she would keep detailed observations of her own teaching performance and her students' oral and written activity during the unit. With the support of her thesis committee and the teacher-research group, she proceeded with her research.

[T]eacher researchers are uniquely positioned to provide a truly emic, or insider's perspective that makes visible the ways that students and teachers together construct knowledge and curriculum. When teachers do research, they draw on interpretive frameworks built from their histories and intellectual interests, and because the research process is embedded in practice, the relationship between knower and known is significantly altered. This obviates the need to "translate findings" in the conventional sense and moves teacher research toward praxis, or critical reflection on practice (Lather, 1986). Furthermore, because teacher researchers often inquire with their students,

students themselves are also empowered as knowers. In this different epistemology, teacher research, currently marginalized in the field, would contribute to a fundamental reconceptualization of the notion of knowledge for teaching. Through inquiry, teachers would play a role in reinventing the conventions of interpretive social science, just as feminist researchers and critical ethnographers have done by making problematic the relationships of researcher and researched, knowledge and authority, and subject and object.

Marilyn Cochran-Smith & Susan L. Lytle, Inside/Outside, p. 43.

Ms. Green planned a six-week unit on *The Color Purple* that would involve (1) conventional teaching strategies, such as discussion and essays; (2) unconventional teaching strategies, such as artistic interpretation of literary relationships; and (3) research-oriented teaching strategies, such as questionnaires that served both as research tools and as instructional vehicles. She wanted these instructional methods to work in concert to enable students to have a rich and varied experience with the novel and to allow her to collect multiple sources of data for her thesis research.

Overall, Ms. Green sought to create a classroom environment in which students felt free to talk openly about their responses to literature and their feelings about classroom processes. She wanted students to leave class with the authority to question what they read and to develop criteria to evaluate why particular books are regarded as "better" than others. She saw *The Color Purple* as an introduction for many students to noncanonical literature, particularly literature written by women and people of color. She also hoped to open her colleagues to curricular possibilities to which they had previously been closed.

To begin their inquiry, Ms. Green felt that students would benefit from some activities to prepare them for both the content of the novel—that is, the issues involved in the characters' relationships—and the form, that being the discourse genre employed by Walker in writing a novel situated in the pre-World War II rural South. The issues were the most controversial problem in teaching the novel, yet to Ms. Green they made it an important and compelling novel to read and study. Prior to their reading, she asked students to bring to class newspaper and magazine clippings that described the issues facing modern society. Students brought articles that reported controversy over sexual identity, incest, domestic violence, racism, gender roles, abuse, and other topics that affected their lives. Ms. Green opened the discussion by asking students to share with the class the content and perspective of these articles. Amy began by volunteering to read an article on domestic violence from a national news magazine that reported that high percentages of American households experience child and spousal abuse. When she was finished, the students discussed the article and their response to the issue:

> *Amy:* I brought this article in because I know people right here at this school who have been abused by their fathers or step-fathers. On the outside you'd never know what's going on because sometimes the families are pretty well off, you know, pillars of the community and all that stuff.

Students apply a wide range of strategies to comprehend, interpret, evaluate, and appreciate texts. They draw on their prior experience, their interactions with other readers and writers, their knowledge of word meaning and other texts, their word identification strategies, and their understanding of textual features (e.g., sound-letter correspondence, sentence structure, context, graphics).

Fred: Now wait a minute. I just saw a *Geraldo* show on domestic abuse and some guy on the show said that some of the stuff that gets counted as domestic abuse is not beating or rape, but stuff like "verbal abuse," which is yelling. Now who can tell me the difference between yelling and verbal abuse?

Carleton: Right. I mean, my mom yells at my dad sometimes. Is that verbal abuse? Or just when a guy does it to a woman? How about if I yell at my brother, which I do all the time? Does that count?

Tammy: Well, that's hard to say. Some of the yelling that goes on is pretty violent. Haven't you ever watched *Oprah?* They have people on all the time who get yelled at, and when you see the guys they look pretty scary.

Carleton: Well sure, but how do you tell the difference?

Melody: Look, if that was the only problem then there'd be no problem. But the truth is that, if anything, domestic abuse is *underreported,* not exaggerated, because women are afraid to report it. And I didn't see that on *Geraldo* or *Hard Copy,* I read it in a magazine.

The class then launched into a discussion of how domestic violence is defined and what its causes and consequences are. This discussion took the rest of the period. Ms. Green realized that she could probably spend much more time on the issue and then spend a few days on the other articles brought in by students, but needed to focus their attention on the relationship between current affairs and *The Color Purple* if the students were to read a broad range of literature during the semester. She therefore told the students that domestic violence, as well as many of the other issues raised in the articles they'd brought in, was among the central conflicts in *The Color Purple,* and that they'd have plenty of opportunities to revisit it in both class discussion and in their writing. By having students begin the unit by identifying the areas of modern life that most affected them, Ms. Green was able to help them approach the novel as a narrative that worked in terms of their own concerns about the world.

In addition to introducing the novel in terms of the issues it raised, Ms. Green felt that the students needed to understand something about the formal features of African American discourse, which few of them spoke at home and which was

Students apply knowledge of language structure, language conventions (e.g., spelling and punctuation), media techniques, figurative language, and genre to create, critique, and discuss print and nonprint texts.

frowned upon and corrected by many teachers throughout the school. Ms. Green knew that an understanding of the distinct features of African American discourse genres would be important for students to appreciate the literary merit of *The Color Purple,* which was often dismissed by critics of multicultural education as relying on "bad" English, thus making it an inferior work of literature that was only granted inclusion in the canon by some curricular affirmative action. She decided to start by introducing students to the art of "signifying" (aka "disin'" or "playing the dozens"), the African American discourse practice consisting of escalating verbal insults that employ a range of ironic and metaphoric devices. Through her reading of *The Color Purple* and attendant literary criticism in her graduate course, she was aware that Alice Walker employed signifying in the development of power relationships among the characters, a critical dimension of human relations when considering domestic violence.

[Signifying is] indirection, circumlocution; metaphorical-imagistic (but images rooted in the everyday, real world); humorous, ironic; rhythmic fluency and sound; teachy but not preachy; directed at person or persons usually present in the situational context (siggers do not talk behind yo back); punning, play on words; introduction of the semantically or logically unexpected.

Geneva Smitherman, *Talkin' and Testifyin',* p. 121.

Ms. Green began by showing several film clips from African American performers such as Sinbad, Eddie Murphy, and others who signify throughout their routines. In doing so she provided the students with familiar examples of the devices employed by Walker in *The Color Purple* to establish the relationships among characters. Students watched the film segments and then worked in small groups to identify the characteristics of the discourse practice. Following their group work they listed as a class the traits of signifying they had identified: use of irony and other figurative language, reliance on insults often aimed at one's mother, intelligence, or other area of personal importance, and use of nonstandard English for emphasis or humor.

Following this introduction to the conventions of signifying, Ms. Green decided to present students with an African American children's story as a way to introduce them to the manner in which signifying can work in literature. She read to the class *Flossie and the Fox* by Patricia C. McKissack, a children's book that she'd read often to her own young child. The story is set in rural Tennessee, and the main character, a young African American girl named Flossie, is asked by her mother to deliver a basket of eggs to her neighbor, whose henhouse has been ravaged by a sly fox. Flossie has never seen a fox before, so she must be wary of any animal who might be the creature in question. Shortly after getting under way, Flossie is followed by an animal who claims to be a fox. He tries to outwit her into giving him the eggs, but Flossie plays on his vanity by signifying on him at every turn, finally tricking him into following her too close to her neighbor's dogs, who voraciously chase him as Flossie skips off to deliver the eggs to her neighbor. The story illustrates, in accessible form, the features of signifying used by the African American comedians they had studied, and by Walker in *The Color Purple*.

Following her reading of *Flossie and the Fox*, Ms. Green asked students to identify the instances of signifying in the story, with an emphasis on examining the ironic and metaphoric quality of the language and their contributions to the quality of Flossie's insults. Students pointed to several examples of signifying in the story:

Jerri: The fox kept on trying to convince her she was a fox, and she kept ignoring him, or whatever. Like, at the beginning he said he was a fox and that she ought to be afraid of him, and she said, "Well, whatever you are, you sho' think a heap of yo'self."

Stacey: Yeah, she knows he's the fox, even though it doesn't say, but she keeps putting him down by saying he's a rabbit or something. At the end the picture shows her smiling, and the book says she knows he's a fox.

Ms. Green: Right. And that's the irony, Flossie saying one thing but believing another.

Rikki: I still have trouble with this irony stuff.

Ms. Green: Well, stick with it and you'll see. Remember that sarcasm is a form of irony, like saying, "Nice dress" if you really think it's ugly. Usually literature is a bit more subtle than that, though, and that's probably why you're having trouble. Now, does anyone else have anything to point out about *Flossie and the Fox?*

Ryan: I liked the part when she felt his fur and said, "Ummm. Feels like rabbit fur to me . . . Shucks! You aine no fox. You a rabbit, all the time trying to fool me." Now that's an insult.

Aspen: Yeah, and the part where he says he's got a long nose so he must be a fox, and she calls him a rat. Read that part again.

Ms. Green: [reads] "Don't prove a thing to me." Flossie picked some wild flowers. "Come to think of it," she said matter-of-fact like, "rats got long pointed noses." She snapped her fingers. "That's it! You a rat trying to pass yo'self off as a fox."

That near 'bout took Fox's breath away. "I beg your pardon," he gasped.

"You can beg all you wanna," Flossie say skipping on down the road. "That still don't make you no fox."

Vanessa: She keeps comparing the fox to little animals like rats and rabbits, so she keeps putting him down.

Ms. Green: How about the language? How does her diction contribute to her insults?

Jake: Well, at least to me it seems more, uh, I don't know, emphatic? Is that the right word? Like there was a part where she compared him to a cat and said something like, "All due respect, Miz Cat, but both y'all got sharp claws and yellow eyes. So . . . that don't prove nothing, 'cep'n both y'all be cats." Like, if she said, "With all respect, Miss Cat, both of you have sharp claws and yellow eyes. So that doesn't prove anything except that both of you are cats." That'd be, I don't know, too proper or something to make a good insult.

Students adjust their use of spoken, written, and visual language (e.g., conventions, style, vocabulary) to communicate effectively with a variety of audiences and for different purposes.

The class then discussed the ways in which her verbal superiority enabled Flossie to triumph over the fox, who was more imposing physically and who regarded himself as the craftier of the two. Peggy pointed out that Flossie's mother cautioned her about the powerful fox at the beginning of the story, yet Flossie's insults weakened his power and put him on the defensive, finally luring him close to the hounds who chased him off into the woods as Flossie skipped off to her neighbor's. Ms. Green noted how the story reminded her of other stories about characters who lack power and must outwit those who try to keep them down. She suggested that the students think about the purpose of signifying in social relations as they read the interactions among characters in *The Color Purple*.

Once they began reading the novel, Ms. Green planned to use discussion as the primary means of exploring the story's meaning. She wanted to use both small-group discussion, which would give everyone a chance to participate and allow students to explore sensitive topics without fear of saying "the wrong thing" for the whole class to judge; and teacher-led class discussions, with the students and Ms. Green moving their chairs to form a circle. Discussion topics would be stimulated by either students' questions and comments about the story, or by their thoughts in response to questions Ms. Green would ask them to write about in journals.

Students employ a wide range of strategies as they write and use different writing process elements appropriately to communicate with different audiences for a variety of purposes.

Journals played a special role in the unit on *The Color Purple*. Ms. Green always encouraged students to keep journals which they could turn in for extra consideration for their class participation grades; she usually didn't require them because some students seemed to get little benefit from keeping them, just going through the motions in order to fulfill the journal assignment, and some were downright hostile to them. For this unit, however, she asked each student to keep a journal. The journal entries served three purposes: to enable students to reflect on their reading, to stimulate class discussions, and to provide data for Ms. Green's thesis research. Students were encouraged to write in their journals outside class and were also provided with specific prompts for in-class entries.

For the in-class journal prompts, Ms. Green wanted students to consider the broader social context that framed their reading of *The Color Purple*. Through her thesis she hoped to understand students' attitudes and the way those attitudes affected their reading; she also wanted to see how their reading and their discussion affected their attitudes. She therefore developed journal prompts that asked students to reflect on their attitudes. Early in the unit, for instance, she posed the question: "Consider literature, film, and television, and the roles typically performed by African American characters. What images are provided to represent African Americans in society?" This question provided a mosaic of student views. Chau-Jih, a Chinese American boy, wrote:

> Mostly on TV I see black people who are poor and live in cities. In movies they are either army sergeants or drug addicts. Black women are mostly mothers on welfare. On the news they mostly interview black people when their apartments burn down or when gang members shoot their children. I guess from this I'd conclude that black people in America are mostly poor and violent, or are in the military, even though I don't think that's true.

Jamie, a white girl, wrote:

> I don't know many black people well, even the ones in my classes. I think they're good at sports. Blacks who are rap singers seem to hate women. Some are doctors like Bill Cosby. I guess they're the same as everybody, but I don't really know.

Terrance, a black male, wrote:

> All you see on TV is black drug addicts and gang members. It really makes me sick. White people own all the TV stations, so what do you expect? I get stopped by the cops all the time just for walking down the street. They all think I've got crack in my pockets because I'm black. You never see normal everyday black people on TV or movies, they're either welfare mothers or gang members or basketball players. According to TV all black people walk around saying "Yo man" and listening to rap music. Did you ever read that cartoon "Doonesbury"? Every black person in it starts every sentence by saying "Yo." You never see people like my parents. My dad's an insurance adjuster and my mom's a math teacher and they have a house in the suburbs. They never say "Yo" and they never watch TV because they hate the way black people are portrayed.

The students used these journal entries to initiate a class discussion on the question that was somewhat tense. Many white students felt uncomfortable sharing their stereotyped views of blacks with their African American classmates, who responded angrily to the first few images that were described. Ms. Green herself was uncomfortable with the discussion. "What am I getting myself into?" she wondered. The resistance from her colleagues was difficult enough to handle; now she faced the prospect of creating new tensions within her classroom.

The discussion, however, opened the floor to students who rarely had spoken during previous discussions that year, and Ms. Green felt encouraged by this new perspective on social issues. She continued to use journal prompts to get students thinking about images of racial groups, and found that over the course of the unit students lost faith in the racial images offered by the media. As data came in for her thesis research, she would turn around and share it with the students, who in turn would want to make it the topic of class discussions and of subsequent journal entries. When Ms. Green analyzed the journal entries and found, for instance, that students typically used words such as "poor," "violent," "drug addicts," "urban," "gang members," and other such negative terms to describe images of African Americans found in the media, they discussed why these images persisted and how they affected non-black people's beliefs about, and behavior towards, African Americans. The discussions were often unsettling to both Ms. Green and the students, but she felt that the

Students apply a wide range of strategies to comprehend, interpret, evaluate, and appreciate texts. They draw on their prior experience, their interactions with other readers and writers, their knowledge of word meaning and other texts, their word identification strategies, and their understanding of textual features (e.g., sound-letter correspondence, sentence structure, context, graphics).

students approached them with more conviction than they usually took toward topics in school.

For her thesis research Ms. Green also wanted to see how students felt about gender roles. At one point she prompted journal writing with the question: "Consider literature, film, and television, and the roles typically performed by women characters. What images are provided to represent women in society?" David wrote:

> Well, women play women. You know, they're wives and stuff. Sometimes there's a character like Murphy Brown, but mostly they're weak, like when they always trip and fall when they're chased in movies and the guy picks them up. TV and movies are pretty much like real life, where men run things. So I don't think girls ought to complain that the images are unfair.

Heather wrote:

> Men get all the strong parts. They're always the doctors, the business executives, the presidents. Have you ever seen a movie where the president of a company is a woman? Even when women play important parts, they're not very appealing. The only women you see in movies who are nice are the ones who go along with what men say. A lot of movies hardly have any women in them at all, or only have women so the men can have girlfriends.

Darlene wrote:

> In books written by men, women are always manipulative and antagonistic, trying to make life difficult for men who are always strong and heroic. If they're not manipulative, the women are really weak victims. In either case the roles are pretty unappealing. But in literature written by women, the women are often victims of oppression, either by men or by society or both, and are usually able to break the oppression. Women write about women who are strong characters. Women writers often show men as narrow-minded and/or violent oppressors. Novels we read in school are always written by men, and men are usually symbols of power and women are symbols of obedience. Men are usually the topics of books and women are only written about when they're part of a man's life. In literature, women's feelings and thoughts are not considered and are never written about. School literature is written from a male's perspective.

These journal entries, and those of the other members of the class, sparked a lively discussion of both the images of women found in popular culture, and the images of women sanctioned by the school curriculum. Boys and girls in the class tended to have different views on the representation of women in American culture. In the discussion, Travis pointed out that women in Arab countries have it much worse, so American women shouldn't complain about their status. This remark prompted much anger among the girls, many of whom spoke sharply to his comments and asserted that the existence of worse conditions didn't justify bad ones. Jason said that he'd never noticed that women are stereotyped in TV, movies, and books; that they seemed to show life as it really is. Sally replied by saying that if the media continue to show the same images, then no one could imagine how things could be different; that the images of women and of African Americans created expectations in people's minds, making it difficult for them to see things other ways. Bart wondered why the girls were so bothered by the sex of the person who wrote a book; what matters, he said, is

Students use spoken, written, and visual language to accomplish their own purposes (e.g., for learning, enjoyment, persuasion, and the exchange of information).

whether it's good or not. Ellen replied that plenty of women were good writers but weren't in the curriculum; if more women wrote the books they read in school, then maybe she'd feel that the curriculum was fair in the way it depicted the genders. Who, she wondered, picks the books that get read in schools? If so many teachers are women, why do they keep choosing books that keep women in their place? And why is it, she wondered, that teachers are mostly women but administrators are all men? Phil complained that with all these feminists around, "It's going to be a lot harder to find a wife to stay home these days than it used to be," a remark that drew a vociferous response from the girls in the class. Hunter said that girls weren't the only ones whose roles were defined by society: "I'm not supposed to cry, or wear pink, or care about people. When things go wrong I'm supposed to act strong and show no signs of weakness. Sometimes I wish I could act more naturally, but I have to act like a man all the time." Some boys rolled their eyes at his comments, but the discussion broadened to recognize the restrictions that social roles placed on all people.

The journal writing and discussion that the students engaged in provided them with a broad social context for their response to the characters in *The Color Purple* and for Ms. Green to monitor their attitudes on social issues for her thesis research. She collected the journals and analyzed them for key words, finding, for instance, that the terms students used to characterize women were "passive," "submissive," "controlled," "victims," "powerless," "quiet," "feminine," "housewives," "on the phone," "insignificant," and other such weak descriptors; while students characterized men as being "powerful," "responsible," "dominating," "protective towards women," "prominent," "aggressive," "decisive," "action-takers," "heroic," and other terms of command. After her analysis she brought her findings back to the students, who discussed these impressions further. She continued to analyze students' journals to see their perceptions of gender images throughout the unit, and found that although many boys were steadfast in their views of gender relations, the class as a whole began to characterize girls with more positive terms.

Ms. Green developed a set of more formal assignments for the students as well, both conventional and unconventional. The primary conventional assignment was an analytic essay that students produced over a two-week period, including small peer-response groups and individual conferences with Ms. Green. The essay allowed students to produce the sort of exposition about the novel that her colleagues required through five-paragraph themes, although Ms. Green structured their writing so that they were more concerned with the content of their writing than with the number of sentences and paragraphs they produced.

To help students find topics, Ms. Green turned to their journals. She found that many students found the topics raised in the novel to be alarming and intriguing, and related to the issues that they had originally brought to class in response to her request for news stories that interested them. Students found that the characters' drug use, experiences with incest, involvement in domestic violence, attitudes towards religion, racial oppression, and other experiences caused them to reflect on their own developing values and principles. Ms. Green's interest in transactional theories of literary response led her to encourage students to write about the novel's social issues and the ways in which they constructed a meaning for them. She hoped to have the topics emerge from the

—— Students read a wide range of literature from many periods in many genres to build an understanding of the many dimensions (e.g., philosophical, ethical, aesthetic) of human experience.

—— Students employ a wide range of strategies as they write and use different writing process elements appropriately to communicate with different audiences for a variety of purposes.

ideas they developed in their journals, and so encouraged students to consult their reflective writing to identify a topic that they would want to pursue in an essay. Students, she found, took different stances toward the novel in their writing. Some students were detached in their writing, standing back from the action and trying to evaluate it dispassionately. Others were more involved, at times talking about the characters as though they were real people, at times projecting themselves into the characters' situations. Either stance lent itself well to formal writing.

She modeled for the students what she might write about herself. She found that the novel's treatment of religion created a lot of ambivalence for her. Religious faith is central to the development of the characters in *The Color Purple*, as it was to Ms. Green herself. Her own religion included a strong missionary spirit that was widely practiced in her church. In the novel, however, white missionaries go to Africa to teach the Olinka tribe about Christianity, and Ms. Green felt uncomfortable about the way in which Walker portrays their efforts as predatory; even while introducing medicine and education to the tribespeople, they simultaneously change their way of life. Ms. Green felt that she would like to write about her feelings in response to this part of the novel. Ms. Green thought aloud with her students about her interests and how she could create a topic from them. She finally found a tentative topic: "What does the novel say about the ways in which cultures control one another through religion and other institutions? To what extent do I agree with Walker's characterization of religion as an instrument of social control?" Through these questions she could explore how Walker treated the issue in the novel, and how she herself saw the issue more broadly in terms of her own experiences and those of others she knew. She assured the students that with such a topic she was not likely to come to a definite resolution to the problem she was exploring, and that in their papers they could conclude with uncertainty if they genuinely remained ambivalent after thinking through the topic.

Students then got in small groups to discuss possible topics, keeping their journals handy to refer to in discussing their interests. For these groups Ms. Green allowed students to work with people of their choice so that they could discuss issues as frankly as possible. Finding a topic was often the easiest part; developing a guiding question was more difficult. Students could say, for instance, that they wanted to write about racism, or gender roles, or some other theme from the book, yet they were often unclear about how to formulate a question clear enough to guide their writing. To help them, Ms. Green took her own research question and turned it into a heuristic that students could adapt to their own interests: "What does the novel say about [a general topic area] and [a specific thing about it]? To what extent do I agree with Walker's characterization of [this specific topic area]?" The heuristic was helpful in getting students started on their questions. Ms. Green scaffolded students' efforts to develop themes by taking the topics of a few students and helping them develop them into questions. Tyrell, for instance, started with "What does the novel say about racial oppression?" but needed to pose a more specific question. Ms. Green asked him what it was that most concerned him about the racial oppression in the novel. Tyrell talked about his general feelings of anger in reading about experiences similar to those his ancestors had gone through, and said that many black people feel that not much has changed. Becky, an Anglo-American student, said in response that things might not be great but that a lot of laws have changed, so it's ridiculous to say that things are exactly the same. Tyrell said that things have changed, but many laws that have changed are not always followed or enforced; why else, he asked, do no black people live in most parts of Fair Oaks? This exchange helped Tyrell pose a more specific question: "What does the novel say about racial oppression and the ways in which people enforce it? To what extent do I agree with Walker's characterization of racial oppression, and is oppression still practiced the same way in today's world?"

Ms. Green helped other students develop their interests into questions to guide their writing, and then had the class return to their small groups to continue developing questions for all the students in the class. She circulated around the room to help students who were stuck or otherwise needed help. When students had questions fully articulated, they could begin writing. Ms. Green encouraged them to use the ideas they'd already developed in their journals to provide the substance of their papers. They could not simply patch together statements from different parts of their journals, but should use those statements as the basis for a new consideration of the problem they'd identified. Students worked on the papers in class and had several days outside class to continue their work.

They then brought drafts in and worked in peer-response groups to receive feedback on their progress. Ms. Green helped to direct their response by providing some guidelines for students to attend to: Does the writer relate all of the various points addressed to the question that frames the inquiry? Does the writer make specific references to the action of the novel in supporting points made? In making a personal judgment about the work's relevance, does the writer go off into deep space, or relate the personal view clearly to the novel and related social issues? Is the writer's language use sufficiently appropriate to communicating effectively with the desired audience?

Students responded to one another's papers and discussed other aspects of their writing they found important. They then had several days in which to revise their papers and turn them in to Ms. Green. To assess the papers, Ms. Green used the same criteria that students used in their small-group response to the writing. Carleton developed the following paper from his journal entries:

The View of Men in *The Color Purple*

In *The Color Purple* Alice Walker portrays women as being under the dominance of men. I didn't realize it before we started discussing this novel, but most women seem to think that men are pretty oppressive characters. If *The Color Purple* is accurate, then men treat women pretty badly for the most part. I don't think all men are the way Alice Walker portrays them, but from what I gather a lot of men were, and still are. First I'll look at the men in the novel, and then I'll talk about the way I see men today.

In *The Color Purple* Celie was beaten and abused by her father, husband, and step-children. I really can't imagine a life like that, but according to some of the girls in class that sort of thing actually happens, even today, and it happens regardless of what race you are. The idea of a father abusing his daughter really makes me sick, but I know just from the newspapers and TV that it happens. Maybe the problem is that Celie didn't have much of an education and so didn't know any better. She just seemed to

Students conduct research on issues and interests by generating ideas and questions, and by posing problems. They gather, evaluate, and synthesize data from a variety of sources (e.g., print and nonprint texts, artifacts, people) to communicate their discoveries in ways that suit their purpose and audience.

assume that that's the way things are and that she didn't have a choice but to put up with it. In a situation like this, whose fault is it, the man's or the woman's? Everyone blames the man, and in this book the man was definitely a problem. But I think that women like Celie should do something to help themselves.

I think that Celie could have stood up for herself more and learned to do something about this problem of men beating her. She acted helpless but there had to be something she could do, like fight back or run away. She needed to be stronger and not give in so easy. She needed more confidence in herself. I just can't imagine being in her shoes and just taking it like that.

The men in the book were really a bunch of losers. I don't know if that's the way it really was back then. Sometimes the author seemed to go too far by making every man totally evil. How did Albert get away with being so mean? I think that there's a lot of male bashing in this world, and this novel seems to present more of it. But the book really made a lot of the girls in the class mad at men, so maybe men are worse than I thought they were. But probably not as totally bad as Alice Walker made them seem.

I have mixed feelings about this book and the way it shows men and women. Today's world is different from the world back then. Women have more opportunities now than they did back then because of Affirmative Action and other laws. Janet Reno even is head of the FBI. Nineties Guys are sympathetic, cry at movies, take care of children, and do other sensitive things. On the other hand, there are still men who abuse their kids, beat their wives, get in fights, start wars, and make other kinds of trouble. And if someone stays at home with the kids, it's usually the woman. As someone once said, the more things change the more they remain the same.

Aside from this formal and informal writing, Ms. Green also provided opportunities for students to produce unconventional interpretations of the novel. One class project was a newspaper that reported the events of the story. Students worked alone or collaborated with others to create newspaper articles, editorials, cartoons, classified advertisements, and other newspaper items that they gathered together for a fictional newspaper about the situations occurring in *The Color Purple*. Preparation for this project came through students' examination of several newspapers to identify the genres of publication they included. Students could choose to contribute whatever they felt capable of producing. Janelle wrote an editorial against child abuse, which Alicia illustrated with an editorial cartoon. Kim and Dennis co-authored an exposé on Albert's treatment of Celie. Hanna wrote a set of personal ads calling for sensitive men seeking long-term relationships. DeMario wrote a review of the film version of *The Color Purple*. Other students produced similar pieces that worked together to make a four-page newspaper that reported on the novel.

The class produced their newspaper on the school's desktop publishing system. They distributed this newspaper in two ways. One was as a literary supplement to the school newspaper, which Ms. Green arranged through her collegial relationship with the school's newspaper advisor. A second means of distribution was to prepare an electronic version of the newspaper which they posted as a file on the school's home page listing on the World Wide Web.

Students adjust their use of spoken, written, and visual language (e.g., conventions, style, vocabulary) to communicate effectively with a variety of audiences and for different purposes.

Students use a variety of technological and informational resources (e.g., libraries, databases, computer networks, video) to gather and synthesize information and to create and communicate knowledge.

Another use of the Internet came about through Ms. Green's connections in the teacher-research group she had joined. Through this group Ms. Green became friends with an English teacher in an urban high school who was also teaching *The Color Purple* at about the same time, and the two set up an Internet connection for students who wished to correspond with one another as pen pals during their reading of the novel. Students could keep their correspondence private, or could save their discussion, print it, and turn it in as a supplement to their journals.

Ms. Green also required a creative project for students to produce, either individually or collaboratively. They could interpret the relationships among characters through any medium of their choice. Ms. Green showed students an excerpt from Disney's animated feature *Fantasia,* in which cartoonists interpret classical music by creating animated stories. She also showed slides of paintings that interpreted historical and Biblical events, played theme songs from movies, discussed movies based on novels, and reviewed other instances of ways in which the message from one medium could be interpreted through another. She devoted class time to allowing students to talk about creative possibilities for interpreting *The Color Purple,* and then told them they had two weeks in which to prepare something to share with the class.

Students ended up producing videotaped dramas, sculptures, paintings, dances, songs, soundtracks, hypertext productions, a claymation film, and other artistic representations of the characters' relationships and experiences. Students shared their creative projects with the class. They also had the option of videotaping their projects and performances and airing them on a special program broadcast on the school's cable television channel.

In my view, if we are to encompass adequately the realm of human cognition, it is necessary to include a far wider and more universal set of competences than has ordinarily been considered. And it is necessary to remain open to the possibility that many—if not most—of these competences do not lend themselves to measurement by standard verbal methods, which rely heavily on a blend of logical and linguistic abilities.

Howard Gardner, *Frames of Mind,* p. x.

For the most part Ms. Green engaged in the same production as her students. As noted, she modeled some of the thinking processes involved in the students' writing, and when she had the time she produced drafts along with them. She maintained a journal of the class's progress for her thesis research, and wrote in it along with the students during in-class journal writing time. When the students were producing their creative projects, Ms. Green, who had no background in the arts, wrote a poem about Celie that she illustrated with an abstract finger painting using materials she borrowed from her own young child. She used the Internet connection to discuss her classroom experiences with her urban counterpart, and referred to those conversations in her classroom discussions with the students, just as she encouraged them to use their pen pals as resources in their discussions. She further took advantage of the Internet by subscribing to a teacher-

— Students use a variety of technological and informational resources (e.g., libraries, databases, computer networks, video) to gather and synthesize information and to create and communicate knowledge.

— Students read a wide range of print and nonprint texts to build an understanding of texts, of themselves, and of the cultures of the United States and the world; to acquire new information; to respond to the needs and demands of society and the workplace; and for personal fulfillment. Among these texts are fiction and nonfiction, classic and contemporary works.

research discussion network, <xtar@listserv.appstate.edu>. Through this network she was able to discuss her research with other teacher-researchers as it was unfolding, getting insights on both the process of her research and the ways it informed her practice.

For her thesis research Ms. Green asked students to respond to questionnaires before, during, and after their study of the novel. These questionnaires often paralleled the themes of the journal prompts. The initial questionnaire asked students to reflect on and evaluate their knowledge of other cultures, of multicultural literature, and of female authors, and their regard for the importance of these issues in their education and personal lives. The second questionnaire asked students to consider their response to *The Color Purple,* their view of the classroom discussions, their understanding of multicultural issues, and related topics; responses were both evaluative and affective. After the unit the students were asked to evaluate its cognitive and affective effects on them, their comfort level in reading and discussing multicultural literature, and their beliefs about the importance of reading noncanonical literature. These questionnaires both provided Ms. Green with data for her thesis and served as the basis for classroom discussions.

Because Ms. Green's classroom research and data collection instruments (e.g., the questionnaires) focused not only on the novel but on the teaching process, discussions addressed both the issues in the literature and the questions about the canon that Ms. Green found so interesting. While boys tended to believe that a book should be chosen for study based strictly on its merit, girls and minority students usually felt that more books that represented their perspective needed to be included in the curriculum. Some students felt that more women and minorities would be included if they were writing better literature; such remarks were challenged by others who felt that white males were controlling the selection process rather than producing superior literature. The discussion of *The Color Purple* thus went beyond the immediate issues presented by the novel and explored the aesthetics of art in general and the politics of curricular planning.

Ms. Green's teaching of the unit, in conjunction with her master's thesis research, enabled her to teach a controversial novel and study its effects on students at the same time. When curious colleagues inquired about the progress of the unit she was able to provide up-to-date reports on how students were managing the material. When a parent called to complain about her feminist agenda, or her "politically correct" instruction, or the sexual content of the literature, she was able to invite the parent in to show the full range of issues covered in their discussions and the ways in which students were making sense of the controversial issues. While some parents were not entirely convinced of the educational justification of the unit, they were satisfied enough not to register discontent with administrators or board members.

The unit occurred late in the year, and so provided a limited foundation for the students' subsequent learning in Ms. Green's class. Nonetheless, themes did emerge that informed their reading during the final quarter and the novel they read, *The Great Gatsby.* Why, asked many students, is this thought to be a "great" book? Who decided that all high school students ought to read it? Why is Daisy so submissive? Why does the curriculum consider a book from the Twenties to be "modern" literature? Ms. Green found that their discussion of

The Great Gatsby continued the interrogation of curriculum and social issues that had begun with *The Color Purple*. She resolved to seek ways to address them earlier in the year in her subsequent teaching.

Standards in Practice

Ms. Green's students, while ordinarily exposed to the standard works of the conventional curriculum, read and consider a noncanonical work of literature in order to consider the moral and aesthetic issues it raises. To approach the work they prepare both through their personal concerns for the modern world and through instruction in a literary genre with which most are unfamiliar. This literary genre requires them to consider new uses of figurative language and language structure and to use this knowledge to inform their response to the literary work. The students use their own reflective writing as the basis for discussion topics, and use their extended consideration of these issues as the basis for their written response to the text. In order to accord the novel due respect, students need to understand the themes it presents and the structure through which it presents them. Both the themes and structure are different from most of what the curriculum offers, and, therefore, require students to enter a new literacy community in order to understand the novel from the inside. Some students take advantage of the Internet to gather and synthesize information and to create and communicate knowledge about social issues and literary response. Through their participation in the discussions, the teacher's research activities, and their writing, the students consider the purposes of schooling and the moral and aesthetic dimensions of literature.

Resources

Curriculum Development

Books

Bloom, A. (1987). *The closing of the American mind: How higher education failed democracy and impoverished the souls of today's children.* New York: Simon & Schuster.

Elbow, P. (1990). *What is English?* Urbana, IL: National Council of Teachers of English.

Farmer, M. (Ed.). (1986). *Consensus and dissent: Teaching English past, present, and future.* Urbana, IL: National Council of Teachers of English.

Glatthorn, A. A. (1980). *A guide for developing an English curriculum for the eighties.* Urbana, IL: National Council of Teachers of English.

Hillocks, G., Jr. (Ed.). (1982). *The English curriculum under fire: What are the real basics?* Urbana, IL: National Council of Teachers of English.

Hirsch, E. D. (1987). *Cultural literacy: What every American needs to know.* Boston: Houghton Mifflin.

Lloyd-Jones, R., & Lunsford, A. (Eds.). (1989). *The English Coalition Conference: Democracy through language.* Urbana, IL: National Council of Teachers of English.

Mandel, B. (1980). *Three language arts curricular models.* Urbana, IL: National Council of Teachers of English.

Mayher, J. S. (1990). *Uncommon sense: Theoretical practice in language education.* Portsmouth, NH: Boynton/Cook Publishers.

Ravitch, D., & Finn, C. E., Jr. (1987). *What do our 17-year-olds know? A report on the first national assessment of history and literature.* New York: Harper & Row.

Simmons, J. S., Shafer, R. E., & West, G. B. (1976). *Decisions about the teaching of English.* Boston: Allyn & Bacon.

Squire, J., & Applebee, R. (1968). *High School English Instruction Today: The national study of high school English programs.* New York: Appleton-Century-Crofts.

Tchudi, S. (1990). *Planning and assessing the curriculum in English language arts.* Alexandria, VA: Association for Supervision & Curriculum Development.

Organizations and Committees

Assembly on Literature for Adolescents of NCTE

NCTE Assembly on American Literature

NCTE Commission on Curriculum

NCTE Committee on Language and Learning Across the Curriculum

NCTE Standing Committee Against Censorship

Gender Issues

Books, Chapters, and Articles

Barbieri, M. (1995). *Sounds from the heart: Learning to listen to girls.* Portsmouth, NH: Heinemann.

Belenky, M. F., Clinchy, B. M., Goldberger, N. R., & Tarule, J. M. (1986). *Women's ways of knowing: The development of self, voice, and mind.* New York: Basic Books.

Biklen, S. K. (1995). *School work: Gender and the cultural construction of teaching.* New York: Teachers College Press.

Bogdan, D. (1992). *Re-educating the imagination: Toward a poetics, politics, and pedagogy of literary engagement.* Portsmouth, NH: Boynton/Cook Publishers.

Davies, B. (1993). *Shards of glass: Children reading and writing beyond gendered identities.* Cresskill, NJ: Hampton Press.

Finders, M. J. (in press). *"Just girls": The literate life and underlife of adolescent girls.* New York: Teachers College Press.

Gabriel, S. L., & Smithson, I. (Eds.). (1990). *Gender in the classroom: Power and pedagogy.* Urbana, IL: University of Illinois Press.

Gaskell, J., & Willinsky, J. (1995). *Gender in/forms curriculum: From enrichment to transformation.* New York: Teachers College Press.

Gilligan, C. (1982). *In a different voice: Psychological theory and women's development.* Cambridge, MA: Harvard University Press.

Jarratt, S., & Worsham, L. (Eds.). (in press). *Feminism and composition.* New York: Modern Language Association.

Kent, T. (1991). *Gender and professional communication.* Special issue of the *Journal of Business and Technical Communication, 5*(4).

Kirsch, G. (1993). *Women writing the academy: Audience, authority, and transformation.* Carbondale, IL: Southern Illinois University Press.

Kopp, C. B., & Kirkpatrick, M. (Eds.). (1979). *Becoming female: Perspectives on development.* New York: Plenum Press.

Lakoff, R. (1990). *Talking power: The politics of language in our lives.* New York: Basic Books.

Langland, E., & Gove, W. (Eds.). (1983). *A feminist perspective in the academy: The difference it makes.* Chicago: University of Chicago Press.

Lloyd, B., & Duveen, G. (1992). *Gender identities and education: The impact of starting school.* London: Harvester Wheatsheaf.

Malinowitz, H. (1995). *Textual orientations: Lesbian and gay students and the making of discourse communities.* Portsmouth, NH: Heinemann.

Martin, J. R. (1992). *The Schoolhome: Rethinking schools for changing families.* Cambridge, MA: Harvard University Press.

Martin, J. R. (1994). *Changing the educational landscape: Philosophy, women, and curriculum.* New York: Routledge.

McCracken, N. M., & Appleby, B. C. (Eds.). (1992). *Gender issues in the teaching of English.* Portsmouth, NH: Boynton/Cook Publishers.

McIntosh, P. (1983). *Interactive phases of curricular re-vision: A feminist perspective.* Wellesley, MA: Wellesley College, Center for Research on Women.

Noddings, N. (1984). *Caring: A feminist approach to ethics and moral education.* Berkeley: University of California Press.

Rubin, D. (1993). *Gender influences: Reading student texts.* Carbondale, IL: Southern Illinois University Press.

Whaley, L., & Dodge, L. (1993). *Weaving in the women: Transforming the high school English curriculum.* Portsmouth, NH: Boynton/Cook Publishers.

Journals

Feminist Studies, Women's Studies Program, University of Maryland
Gender and Society, Sage Publications
Radical Teacher, P.O. Box 102, Cambridge, MA 02141

Organizations and Committees

NCTE Assembly on Gay and Lesbian Academic Issues Awareness
NCTE Committee on the Status of Women in the Profession (subcommittee of the Conference on College Composition and Communication)
NCTE Women in Literature and Life Assembly

World Wide Web Sites

http://www.cybergrrl.com
http://www.women.com

Censorship

Books and Pamphlets

ALA. (1991). *Intellectual freedom for children: A packet of materials* (Rev. ed.). Chicago: The Association for Library Service to Children.

ALA. (1992). *Intellectual Freedom Manual* (4th ed.). Chicago: American Library Association.

Brown, J. E. (Ed.). (1994). *Preserving intellectual freedom: Fighting censorship in our schools.* Urbana, IL: National Council of Teachers of English.

Burress, L., & Jenkinson, E. B. (1982). *The students' right to know.* Urbana, IL: National Council of Teachers of English.

Chion-Kenney, L. (1989). *Censorship: Managing the controversy.* Alexander, VA: National School Board Association.

Davis, J. E. (Ed.). (1979). *Dealing with censorship.* Urbana, IL: National Council of Teachers of English.

DelFattore, J. (1992). *What Johnny shouldn't read: Textbook censorship in America.* New Haven, CT: Yale University Press.

Foerstel, H. N. (1994). *Banned in the U.S.A.: A reference guide to book censorship in schools and public libraries.* Westport, CT: Greenwood Press.

Ingelhart, L. E. (1986). *Press law and press freedom for high school publications: Court cases and related decisions discussing free expression guarantees and limitations for high school and journalists.* New York: Greenwood Press.

Jenkinson, E. (1986). *The schoolbook protest movement: 40 questions & answers.* Bloomington, IN: Phi Delta Kappa Educational Foundation.

Karolides, N. J., & Burress, L. (Eds.). (1985). *Celebrating censored books!* Racine, WI: Wisconsin Council of Teachers of English.

Moffett, J. (1988). *Storm in the mountains: A case study of censorship, conflict, and consciousness.* Carbondale, IL: Southern Illinois University Press.

Ochoa, A. (Ed.). (1990). *Academic freedom to teach and to learn.* Washington, D.C.: National Education Association.

People for the American Way. *Attacks on freedom to learn.* Annual Reports. Washington, D.C.: People for the American Way.

Reichman, H. (1988). *Censorship and selection: Issues and answers for schools.* Chicago: American Library Association; and Arlington, VA: American Association of School Administrators.

Simmons, J. S. (1994). *Censorship: A threat to reading, learning, and thinking.* Newark, NJ: International Reading Association.

Task Force on Guidelines for Dealing with Censorship on Nonprint Materials. (1983). *Guidelines for dealing with censorship of nonprint materials.* Urbana, IL: National Council of Teachers of English.

West, M. I. (1988). *Trust your children: Voices against censorship in children's literature.* New York: Neal-Schuman Publishers.

Videos

Carter, H. *Inside story.* Alexandria, VA: PBS Video.

Moyers, B. *Bill Moyers: The public mind.* Alexandria, VA: PBS Video.

Organizations and Committees

ALA Office for Intellectual Freedom, Chicago, IL

Fairness & Accuracy in Reporting (FAIR), New York, NY

National Coalition against Censorship, New York, NY

NCTE Conference on English Education's Conference on Intellectual Freedom

NCTE Standing Committee Against Censorship

NCTE/SLATE Steering Committee on Social & Political Concerns

People for the American Way, Washington, D.C.

Teacher Research

Books and Articles

Altrichter, H. (1993). *Teachers investigate their work: An introduction to the methods of action research.* New York: Routledge.

Atwell, N. (1987). *In the middle: Writing, reading, and learning with adolescents.* Upper Montclair, NJ: Boynton/Cook Publishers.

Bissex, G., & Bullock, R. (Eds.). (1987). *Seeing for ourselves: Case study research by teachers of writing.* Portsmouth, NH: Heinemann.

Cochran-Smith, M., & Lytle, S. L. (Eds.). (1993). *Inside/outside: Teacher research and knowledge.* New York: Teachers College Press.

Corey, S. M. (1953). *Action research to improve school practices.* New York: Bureau of Publications, Teachers College, Columbia University.

Daiker, D., & Morenberg, M. (Eds.). (1990). *The writing teacher as researcher: Essays in the theory and practice of class-based research.* Portsmouth, NH: Boynton/Cook Publishers.

Eisenhart, M. A. (1993). *Designing classroom research: Themes, issues, and struggles.* Boston: Allyn & Bacon.

Filby, N. N. (1991). *An action research approach to authentic curriculum and instruction.* San Francisco, CA: Far West Laboratory for Education Research and Development.

Fleischer, C. (1995). *Composing teacher-research: A prosaic history.* Albany, NY: State University of New York Press.

Gallas, K. (1994). *The languages of learning: How children talk, write, dance, draw, and sing their understanding of the world.* New York: Teachers College Press.

Goswami, D., & Stillman, P. (Eds.). (1987). *Reclaiming the classroom: Teacher research as an agency for change.* Upper Montclair, NJ: Boynton/Cook Publishers.

Hollingsworth, S. (1994). *Teacher research and urban literacy education: Lessons and conversations in a feminist key.* New York: Teachers College Press.

Hubbard, R. S., & Power, B. M. (Eds.). (1991). *Literacy in process: Resource guide for teachers.* Portsmouth, NH: Heinemann.

Hubbard, R. S., & Power, B. M. (1993). *The art of classroom inquiry: A handbook for teacher-researchers.* Portsmouth, NH: Heinemann.

Lensmire, T. (1994). *When children write: Critical re-visions of the writing workshop.* New York: Teachers College Press.

Lott, J. G. (1994). *A teacher's stories: Reflections on high school writers.* Portsmouth, NH: Boynton/Cook Publishers.

McKernan, J. (1991). *Curriculum action research: A handbook of methods and resources for the reflective practitioner.* New York: St. Martin's Press.

Mohr, M. M., & MacLean, M. S. (1987). *Working together: A guide for teacher-researchers.* Urbana, IL: National Council of Teachers of English.

Myers, M. (1985). *The teacher-researcher: How to study writing in the classroom.* Urbana, IL: National Council of Teachers of English.

Noffke, S. E., & Stevenson, R. B. (Eds.). (1995). *Educational action research: Becoming practically critical.* New York: Teachers College Press.

Patterson, L., Santa, C., Short, K., & Smith, K. (Eds.). (1993). *Teachers are researchers: Reflection and action.* Newark, DE: International Reading Association.

Porter, A. C. (1986). *Collaborating with teachers on research: Pioneering efforts at the Institute for Research on Teaching.* East Lansing, MI: Institute for Research on Teaching, Michigan State University.

Ray, R. E. (1993). *The practice of theory: Teacher research in composition.* Urbana, IL: National Council of Teachers of English.

Richardson-Koehler, V. (1988). *The use of practical arguments in staff development: A study of teachers' research-based instruction of reading comprehension.* Tucson, AZ: College of Education, University of Arizona.

Shanahan, T. (Ed.). (1994). *Teachers thinking, teachers knowing: Reflections on literacy and language education.* Urbana, IL: National Council of Teachers of English and National Conference on Research in English.

Smagorinsky, P., & Jordahl, A. (1991). The student teacher/cooperating teacher collaborative study: A new source of knowledge. *English Education, 23*(1), 54–59.

Stock, P. L. *The dialogic curriculum: Teaching and learning in a multicultural society.* Portsmouth, NH: Heinemann.

Winter, R. (1987). *Action-research and the nature of social inquiry: Professional innovation and educational work.* Brookfield, VT: Gower Publishing Company.

Journals

Cambridge Journal of Education, University of Cambridge, Institute of Education

Curriculum Studies, Wilfred Carr, Division of Education, 388 Glossop Road, Sheffield, S10 2JA, England

Educational Action Research, Centre for Applied Research in Education, University of East Anglia

International Journal of Qualitative Studies in Education, University of Tennessee

The Journal of Teaching and Learning, North Dakota Study Group Center for Teaching & Learning, University of North Dakota

Language Arts, National Council of Teachers of English

New Schools, New Communities: Voices for Educational Change, Scott Thompson, Institute for Responsive Education, 605 Commonwealth Avenue, Boston, MA 02215

Primary Voices, National Council of Teachers of English

Reading Teacher, International Reading Association, Kent, OH

Rethinking Schools, Rethinking Schools, Milwaukee, WI

Teacher Research: The Journal of Classroom Inquiry, University of Maine

Teachers and Teaching, University of Nottingham

Teaching and Learning: The Journal of Natural Inquiry, Center for Teaching and Learning, University of North Dakota

Workshop: By and for Teachers, Heinemann

E-mail Network

xtar@listserv.appstate.edu

Prior Knowledge and Literature

Books

Johannessen, L. R. (1992). *Illumination rounds: Teaching the literature of the Vietnam War.* Urbana, IL: National Council of Teachers of English.

Kahn, E., Walter, C. C., & Johannessen, L. R. (1984). *Writing about literature.* Urbana, IL: ERIC Clearinghouse on Reading and Communication Skills and National Council of Teachers of English.

Lee, C. D. (1993). *Signifying as a scaffold for literary interpretation: The pedagogical implications of an African American discourse genre.* NCTE Research Report No. 26. Urbana, IL: National Council of Teachers of English.

Rabinowitz, P. (1987). *Before reading: Narrative conventions and the politics of interpretation.* Ithaca, NY: Cornell University Press.

Robinson, R. (1988). *Unlocking Shakespeare's language: Help for the teacher and student.* Urbana, IL: ERIC Clearinghouse on Reading and Communication Skills and National Council of Teachers of English.

Smagorinsky, P., McCann, T., & Kern, S. (1987). *Explorations: Introductory activities for literature and composition, grades 7–12.* Urbana, IL: ERIC Clearinghouse on Reading and Communication Skills and National Council of Teachers of English.

Smith, M. W. (1991). *Understanding unreliable narrators: Reading between the lines in the literature classroom.* Urbana, IL: National Council of Teachers of English.

Teaching African American Literature

Books

Brown, D. H. (1994). *Multicultural literature in the classroom: A study of The Color Purple.* Unpublished master's thesis, the University of Oklahoma.

Campbell, J. (1986). *Mythic black fiction: The transformation of history.* Knoxville, TN: University of Tennessee Press.

Cooper, A. (1988, 1892). *A voice from the South by a black woman of the South.* New York: Oxford University Press.

Davies, C. B. (1994). *Black women, writing, and identity: Migrations of the subject.* New York: Routledge.

Gates, H. L. (1988). *The signifying monkey: A theory of Afro-American literary criticism.* New York: Oxford University Press.

Hale-Benson, J. E. (1982). *Black children: Their roots, culture, and learning styles.* Provo, UT: Brigham Young University Press.

Johnson, D. (1990). *Telling tales: The pedagogy and promise of African American literature for youth.* New York: Greenwood Press.

Kochman, T. (1972). *Rappin' and stylin' out: Communication in urban black America.* Urbana, IL: University of Illinois Press.

Labov, W. (1972). *Language in the inner city: Studies in the black English vernacular.* Philadelphia, PA: University of Pennsylvania Press.

Lee, C. D. (1993). *Signifying as a scaffold for literary interpretation: The pedagogical implications of an African American discourse genre.* NCTE

Research Report No. 26. Urbana, IL: National Council of Teachers of English.

McKissack, P. C. (1986). *Flossie & the fox*. New York: Dial Books for Young Readers.

Smith, V. (1987). *Self-discovery and authority in Afro-American narrative*. Cambridge, MA: Harvard University Press.

Smitherman, G. (1977). *Talkin' and testifyin': The language of black America*. Boston: Houghton Mifflin; Reprint, Detroit: Wayne University Press, 1986.

Wright, L. A. (1995). *Identity, family, and folklore in African American literature*. New York: Garland Publications.

Relating Arts and Language Arts

Books and Articles

Blandy, D., & Congdon, K. G. (Eds.). (1987). *Art in a democracy*. New York: Teachers College Press.

Christenbury, L. (Ed.). (1995). *Multiple intelligences*. Special theme issue of *English Journal, 84*(8).

Dewey, J. (1934). *Art as experience*. New York: Minton, Balch, & Company.

Gardner, H. (1983). *Frames of mind: The theory of multiple intelligences*. New York: Basic Books.

Gardner, H. (1993). *Multiple intelligences: The theory into practice* (2nd ed.). New York: Basic Books.

Goodman, N. (1976). *Languages of art: An approach to a theory of symbols*. Indianapolis: Hackett Publishing Company.

Greene, M. (1978). *Landscapes of learning*. New York: Teachers College Press.

John-Steiner, V. (1985). *Notebooks of the mind: Explorations of thinking*. Albuquerque, NM: University of New Mexico Press.

Moody, W. J. (Ed.). (1990). *Artistic intelligences: Implications for education*. New York: Teachers College Press.

Naumburg, M. (1973). *An introduction to art therapy: Studies of the "free" art expression of behavior problem children and adolescents as a means of diagnosis and therapy*. New York: Teachers College Press.

Shuman, R. B., & Wolfe, D. (1990). *Teaching English through the arts*. Urbana, IL: National Council of Teachers of English.

Smagorinsky, P. (1991). *Expressions: Multiple intelligences in the English class*. Urbana, IL: National Council of Teachers of English.

Smagorinsky, P. (1995). Constructing meaning in the disciplines: Reconceptualizing writing across the curriculum as composing across the curriculum. *American Journal of Education, 103*(2), 160–184.

Smagorinsky, P., & Coppock, J. (1994). Cultural tools and the classroom context: An exploration of an alternative response to literature. *Written Communication, 11*(3), 283–310.

Smagorinsky, P., & Coppock, J. (1995). The reader, the text, the context: An exploration of a choreographed response to literature. *JRB: A Journal of Literacy, 27*(3), 271–298.

Suhor, C. (1984). Towards a semiotics-based curriculum. *Journal of Curriculum Studies, 16*(3), 247–257.

Suhor, C. (1994). Semiotics. In A. Purves (Ed.), *Encyclopedia of English Studies and Language Arts* (pp. 1068–1070). Urbana, IL: National Council of Teachers of English and Scholastic.

Vygotsky, L. S. (1971). *The psychology of art* (Scripta Technica, Trans.). Cambridge, MA: MIT Press.

Walker, P. P. (1993). *Bring in the arts: Lessons on dramatics, art, and story writing for elementary and middle-school classrooms.* Portsmouth, NH: Heinemann.

Organizations and Committees

NCTE Assembly on Expanded Perspectives of Learning

NCTE Assembly on Media Arts

Project Zero, Harvard University

Electronic Mail Networks

These networks discuss teaching issues.

    ncte-talk@itc.org

    english-teachers@ux1.cso.uiuc.edu

This network serves divisions of the American Educational Association.

    listserv@asu.edu

This network discusses semiotics based on the work of Charles Sanders Peirce.

    listproc@unicorn.acs.ttu.edu

This network discusses modern applications of John Dewey's "progressive" movement in education.

    dewey-L@ux1.cso.uiuc.edu

CHAPTER FIVE

COMING TO AMERICA

Daphne Watson taught in Lincoln High School, a four-year school of about 2,000 students. Lincoln High occupied an aging building in the industrial section of a Midwestern city. The sounds of traffic and factory machinery provided a steady background for Daphne Watson's teaching and students' learning, rattling through the security bars and chipped window frames that occupied the exterior wall of her classroom. Beneath the windows steam radiators hissed and clanked throughout the long winters, adding another layer of noise to the cacophony.

The school was a neighborhood comprehensive high school; that is, it was not one of the city's "magnet" schools: it had no special programs to attract students from other parts of the city, but only served the immediate community surrounding it. Typically about one-fifth of Lincoln's graduating class went on to college or trade school, mostly to one of the city's colleges or junior colleges; fewer than half of these students ended up earning degrees from four-year colleges. Many students worked at entry-level, blue-collar jobs after school, and often sought full-time work in the neighborhood's factories or small businesses upon graduation.

The students of Lincoln High were, as many faculty members joked, a "United Nations" of races and ethnicities. The racial breakdown was 40% white, 20% African American, 15% Latino/a, 15% Asian American, and 10% Native American. Among these racial groups there was considerable ethnic diversity. A great many students were first, second, or third generation Americans who lived in the same neighborhoods as their extended families. The closeness of extended families was helped by the homogeneous makeup of the city's neighborhoods. The city as a whole tended to be voluntarily segregated, with such areas as Chinatown, Little Italy, Greektown, and other ethnic enclaves easily identifiable through clusters of restaurants, markets, and other culturally distinct businesses.

Ms. Watson taught in a department of fifteen English teachers. Like most of her colleagues on the faculty, she was a white female. Her teaching assignment included two sections of basic-track sophomores, one section of drama, and two sections of regular-track juniors. Class size typically ranged from twenty-five to thirty students, with no aides or parent volunteers to help with management, instruction, or grading papers. In addition to her teaching, Ms. Watson supervised a study hall of eighty students and had one period of hall duty every day. After school she served as the director of the school's plays, which featured one performance in each of the school-year's four marking periods. She was also required to chaperon at least one school-sponsored extracurricular event each marking period.

Ms. Watson taught within a clearly prescribed curriculum that was developed through the city's central curriculum office by a group of teachers and administrators representing each school in the district. The curriculum tended to follow the organization of the commercially produced anthologies and textbooks that the district purchased. The sophomore curriculum followed the textbook's "genre" format, with each marking period centered on one or two specific genres: first short stories, then poems, then drama, and finally novels and nonfiction prose. The junior curriculum covered American literature chronologically, starting with the Puritans, colonial literature, and Native American legends, and moving forward through time to the mid-twentieth century.

Ms. Watson did not particularly like either of these two means of organization, but needed to adhere to them with reasonable faithfulness in order to maintain good relations with her administrators and colleagues. According to the school administration, if she were to teach literary selections or parts of speech out of order, she would make the transition difficult for the students who changed their schedules in mid-term. She also needed to make sure to teach specific literary works at the agreed-upon point in the curriculum; early in her career she had taught Crane's "The Open Boat," one of the staples of the junior curriculum, to her sophomores and had been disparaged at a department meeting by a colleague who felt that her own teaching of the story the following year had been violated by the students' prior exposure to the work.

Her discomfort with the curriculum came from the restrictions it placed on her decision making. The genre format of the sophomore curriculum made it difficult for her to combine various works into thematic units; and the chronological approach of the junior year, while allowing for some thematic grouping, mitigated against grouping selections from the anthology across eras. Furthermore, the junior curriculum started the year with Puritan and colonial texts that most students found remote and archaic, thus making her goal of engaging students with literature difficult.

Beyond the problems of the chronological sequence, Ms. Watson had always found the content of the American literature curriculum to be unsatisfying. While offering an excellent set of selections from the traditional canon and reinforcing many of the values that were central to the development of mainstream American culture, the anthology-based curriculum did not reflect the full range of experiences and perspectives that her students brought to class. Her Asian students, for instance, included Laotian, Cambodian, Korean, and Chinese immigrants whose contributions to American culture were rarely addressed in the traditional canon of American literature, because either the traditional canon was well established and difficult to displace or because the ethnic groups' relocations were too recent to be represented. She saw similar problems with other groups of students who had a difficult time finding a purpose for reading the experiences and viewpoints of the Puritans and other early colonists. The curriculum worked well for some of her students, but was problematic for many, leading Ms. Watson to consider other ways to approach it.

Unhappy with both her own experiences with the course and those of her students, Ms. Watson decided to make some changes in her approach. In reflecting on why she had become an English teacher in the first place, she thought of the many books she had curled up with since her childhood and the ways in which she found them insightful about the human condition. Yet in the school curriculum, literature often was presented as an object to study, not as a means for students to consider and make sense of their worlds. The problems of the approach to literature assumed by her curriculum were perhaps epitomized by the factual questions that were scripted in her teacher's manual, questions that rarely spoke to her students' purposes for reading. Daphne Watson believed that literature should serve as a stimulus for students to help them think about themselves, their own worlds, and the more exotic worlds presented by authors. The way the curriculum was presented, it seemed to provide little for students to respond to in terms of their own personal interests, and did not sufficiently engage students to help them think about other perspectives on the world. During her previous efforts to teach American literature, she had been struck by her students' inability to see the ways in which the colonial experience was a reflection of their own histories. By making changes, she hoped to enable students to see that colonial literature, while written in what registered to them as antiquated language, contained themes that spoke to the experiences of the many and varied American immigrant groups.

The Puritans, for instance, had left England to escape religious harassment and attempted to set up a new community in a new land. Many subsequent immigrant groups had similarly been persecuted at home and emigrated to escape and begin a new life. Rebecca, for example, was a fourth-generation Byelorussian Jew whose grandparents had immigrated to America in 1915 to escape the pogroms that were exterminating Jews throughout Eastern Europe at the time. Huong was a Cambodian who, as a young child, had been crammed aboard a crude seacraft by his parents in the hopes that he would escape the death squads of Pol Pot that were sweeping across their land. He ended up sailing across the world and being relocated to this Midwestern city, living with extended family members who had fled in the same manner. Many of Ms. Watson's other students were from families who had escaped similar oppression, or who had left economically destitute circumstances and seen America as a New World in which to start afresh.

In addition, there were two other groups of students at Lincoln High School who were affected by the European settlement of America: Native Americans and African Americans. The Puritan story, while a celebration of the opportunities offered to oppressed Europeans by the New World, was viewed quite differently by the Native American students in Ms. Watson's class, who saw European immigration as the beginning of the end of their ancestors' way of life. The African American students saw the Jamestown settlement as the beginning of the plantation society that created new markets for African slaves, and, thus, as the impetus for their own tragic history.

These various perspectives were often refracted by her students' cultural ambivalence. Ms. Watson was aware that the history of immigration was more complex than simple racial or continental divisions could account for. The early Spanish, French, Dutch, and English explorers—typically lumped together as Europeans—were not unified, but competed with one another, often in armed conflict, for New World resources. Many Native American tribes had been at war with one another for centuries, and some forged alliances with European traders and their superior weaponry to help win their intraracial battles. Some early groups of explorers consisted entirely of men, and, as a consequence, were more likely to intermarry with indigenous people and develop relatively harmonious relationships. The African slave trade was primarily an Arab enterprise, and New World settlers copied Arab methods by enslaving conquered native people and selling them throughout the Caribbean. Finally, Daphne Watson knew that few people had a "pure" heritage, but were mixtures of many cultures. Her understanding of the culturally complex heritages of American citizens led her to seek a more complex way of studying American literature.

As she thought about her students in relation to the curriculum, Ms. Watson began to see possibilities of an approach that would help them see more personal meaning in their studies and, consequently, produce more substantial academic work. She therefore decided to recast the colonial period as a "Coming to America" unit that focused on the complexity of the colonial period and also allowed students to explore their own involvement in the history of American immigration. She decided that she could help her students meet the district's writing goals—and help students synthesize their understanding of colonial settlement and their own position in American history—by having them produce a research project on their families' and cultural groups' experiences with immigration.

What you teach, teach thoroughly.

Alfred North Whitehead, *The Aims of Education*, p. 2.

The unit she conceived included both an introduction to the unit's themes and a subsequent research project related to those themes. She viewed the introductory activity as a means for the whole class to consider the possibility that history, including the history of immigration, may be viewed from many perspectives. For the introduction, Ms. Watson seized on an unexpected opportunity provided by mass media. The summer before she planned to teach the "Coming to America" unit, Disney released its animated version of *Pocahontas*. The film was roundly criticized by conservative commentators as promoting a revisionist "politically correct" version of the traditional Pocahontas story, forwarding a political agenda that undermined white male institutions and perpetuated "the politics of guilt." Ms. Watson became fascinated by the controversy surrounding the film and began reading about Pocahontas. Through her research she found that there was no authoritative version of the story; even John Smith, the primary source of the tale, had told it in different ways on different occasions. Subsequently, there were many different versions of the story that different people had developed over time in order to represent their own interests. She decided that she could introduce the "Coming to America" theme by selecting several versions of the Pocahontas tale and having students study them to understand the vision of America represented by each, and subsequently to see that perspectives on history—including immigration—differ depending on the values, experiences, and agendas of the historian.

Students read a wide range of print and nonprint texts to build an understanding of texts, of themselves, and of the cultures of the United States and the world; to acquire new information; to respond to the needs and demands of society and the workplace; and for personal fulfillment. Among these texts are fiction and nonfiction, classic and contemporary works.

She began by asking each student to write down the "true" Pocahontas story as he or she understood it. Although some students were fuzzy on the details, most had a basic knowledge of the story, at least in terms of Pocahontas saving John Smith from death at the hands of Powhatan. Michael, the son of Greek immigrants, wrote:

> I didn't see the Pocahontas movie so I'm not sure I know the whole story. I think Pocahontas was an Indian who lived with her tribe, the Powhatans. Her father was the chief. I think his name was Powhatan too. They lived in either Masachusets or Virginia, I forget which one. John Smith was sent by the king of England to go to America to find gold and furs. He was the captain of his ship and was very brave. They got to America and build a fort. I don't think he was a Puritan because I don't think he dressed funny so maybe it was Virginia. They tried to survive in their fort but the Indians kept attacking them. Somehow John Smith got caught by the Powhatans and they tried to kill him but Pocahontas ran in and saved him so he lived and they became friends and the Indians taught the settlers how to grow corn so they survived after all.

When the students were finished writing their stories, Ms. Watson asked them to get in small groups to compare their versions. She usually allowed students to get in groups of their choice, because she believed that they worked better with friends than with people they were assigned to work with. For this assignment, however, she assigned the group memberships, selecting people of different backgrounds and outlooks to work together because she hoped to see variety in the perspectives of the stories they wrote.

As she anticipated, each group had diverse representations of the story. There was variety in students' knowledge of the story line. Some knew that after marrying John Rolfe, Pocahontas had gone to England, met the queen, and died of illness shortly thereafter at the age of twenty-one. Others thought she had married John Smith and stayed on her own continent. Others knew she had married John Rolfe but were not quite sure how she had made the transition from Smith to Rolfe, or what she had done with her life following her marriage.

There was also variety in the perspectives that students took on the story. Some adopted the perspective of the Powhatans and viewed the Europeans as trespassers and usurpers, generally portraying them as greedy and exploitative. Ms. Watson was not surprised that her Native American students took this view, as did some other students who had seen the Disney film or whose sympathies lay with the conquered. Such students had mixed views of Pocahontas, some seeing her as a dupe of the explorers, others as a peacemaker between two incompatible ways of life, and others as a young fool who sowed the seeds of her own destruction. Other students regarded the Native Americans as "savages" who threatened the lives of the more civilized European explorers, and regarded Pocahontas as a saintly figure whose rescue of John Smith revealed her enlightenment and recognition of the superiority of English culture and technology.

Ms. Watson provided students with the following set of questions, had them get into their groups, and asked each group to use the questions to identify the perspective of each group member's version.

1. Which events of the story are presented in this account of the tale, and how are the characters depicted in these events? What does the selection

Students read a wide range of print and nonprint texts to build an understanding of texts, of themselves, and of the cultures of the United States and the world; to acquire new information; to respond to the needs and demands of society and the workplace; and for personal fulfillment. Among these texts are fiction and nonfiction, classic and contemporary works.

Students apply knowledge of language structure, language conventions (e.g., spelling and punctuation), media techniques, figurative language, and genre to create, critique, and discuss print and nonprint texts.

of events and portrayal of characters reveal about the perspective of the storyteller? What values is the storyteller conveying—intentionally or unintentionally—through the qualities portrayed through the characters and their actions?

2. How "accurate" is the story? What does it mean to be "accurate" when reporting history?

Michael was assigned to a group that included three other students: Jabari, Imelda, and Luis. After looking at Michael's rendition of the story, the students engaged in the following discussion of his narrative:

Jabari: Well, looks like this is mostly about John Smith.

Michael: Hey, I wrote what I could remember, alright?

Imelda: Right, that's what you're supposed to do. And now we're supposed to talk about how you told the story.

Luis: OK, what's the first question, "Which events of the story are presented in this account of the tale, and how are the characters depicted in these events?" Well, Michael talks about John Smith coming over and building a fort and getting caught and getting saved by Pocahontas and then surviving. Jabari's right, this is mostly about John Smith.

Imelda: Yeah, Pocahontas only comes in at the end.

Jabari: Looks like you're telling this from John Smith's point of view since that's who you talk about.

Imelda: Right, look what you say at the end, the settlers survive. In the movie the story is about how the settlers are wrong, and at the end they lock up their leader for exploiting everybody.

Luis: So, Michael, it looks like you're on the side of the settlers here.

Michael: What's wrong with that? Just because the movie's on one side doesn't mean that I'm wrong.

Jabari: Hey, no problem, our job is to see whose side you're on, not to see who's right. Now let's see, what next? I'd say that Michael here is on the side of the settlers, and we've already said why.

Imelda: You sure forgot a lot of the details.

Michael: Hey, give me a break. I told you I didn't see the movie.

Luis: Well that's probably enough for Michael. Let's try someone else. . . .

Following the small-group analyses of their stories, the students came together as a class to share their findings and discuss the problem of perspective in historical writing. After looking at various versions of the story, the class discussed the idea of historical perspectives.

Ms. Watson: Well, what do you think history is? We have history books and they tell us what happened in the past. Are history books always right?

Ted: Sometimes history books tell the same story in different ways. When I was a kid I lived in the South. We studied the Civil War, and all the pictures of John Brown in our history book were really wild looking, you know, crazy beard and bugged out eyes, and the books described him like a nut. Then I moved up here and studied the Civil War, and John

Students use spoken, written, and visual language to accomplish their own purposes (e.g., for learning, enjoyment, persuasion, and the exchange of information).

Students apply knowledge of language structure, language conventions (e.g., spelling and punctuation), media techniques, figurative language, and genre to create, critique, and discuss print and nonprint texts.

Brown was described as a hero for being an abolitionist. So I can tell you that not all history books tell the same story the same way.

Imelda: How about things that are happening right now? Did you see the trial on TV last summer? I watched it every day when I wasn't working. Some witnesses tell it one way, some tell it another. Sometimes the same witness will say different things depending on the question. It's really hard to tell what really happened in this trial. I think maybe the rest of history's the same.

Yong: But in the trial people got paid to testify, so they tell the story the way the lawyers want. History books aren't written by paid witnesses.

Ted: Yeah, but history books are written by people, and people see things differently.

Isabel: I was just going to say that everyone's got an opinion, but some opinions are better than others. I mean, some people check the facts, and other people just say what they think, or they just say what they want you to believe.

Lucas: Right, some people just tell the facts of what happens, and some people change them so they get their way. I think history books just tell the facts and don't put their opinions in.

The discussion continued in this fashion, becoming energetic and at times heated as students considered the question of a "real" Pocahontas story and also raised questions about other historical events, such as whether or not there was a Holocaust, whether or not the Bible is literally true, and other problems related to the question of whether history is an objective or subjective account of the past. Students whose families had recently escaped Indochina reported the ways in which their governments provided "official" versions of history that supported their own interests, therefore raising questions about the authenticity of recorded history. Other students responded by saying that such government control could only come in totalitarian countries, but not in America. One student whose father was a labor organizer in his factory said that the union's recent strike was reported very differently in the city newspaper than in the union newspaper, supporting the idea that history can be told from different angles. Other students responded that his union newspaper had the interests of union members to protect and so distorted the facts, while the city newspaper was more objective and, therefore, more likely to be telling the true story. Ms. Watson found that the students had plenty to say on the topics, making her role more an orchestrator than a director of the discussion.

Following this discussion the class returned to the issue of Pocahontas by analyzing a set of published versions of the story. In a manner similar to their study of their own stories, students were given several different books about Pocahontas that Ms. Watson had checked out from the library, and were asked the same questions they had answered about their own versions.

Students discussed the stories in groups, using the questions as guidelines. Jabari, Imelda, Luis, and Michael got back together and looked at two books, the *Pocahontas* book by Disney based on the movie, and *Pocahontas, Girl of Jamestown* by Kate Jassem. The books were considerably longer than their own narratives, providing many more details for them to consider in determining the narrator's perspective. They found that the Disney version told the story from the Native American perspective, and that Jassem's book took the perspective of the settlers.

Rather than following the small-group discussions with a class discussion, Ms. Watson asked each student to select one version of the story that they'd read and write an analysis of it, using the ideas exchanged in their discussions as the basis of their essays. Through this assignment Ms. Watson was able to meet one of the requirements of the writing curriculum, the production of an argumentative essay. She reviewed with students some of the traits of such writing: for each claim they made, they needed to provide evidence in the form of an example from the story, and needed to explain why the example illustrated the claim. They also needed to anticipate how someone would disagree with their claim and rebut the objection. Ms. Watson pointed out that in their small-group discussions of the stories they had gone through all of these processes. For their writing they needed to reconsider the content of the small-group discussions and take a position in their writing. To provide a concrete guideline for the students, she prepared an outline of the points they needed to include to develop a persuasive argument, with an illustration from their previous class discussion on their own versions of the Pocahontas tale:

Arguing a Point

To persuade someone of your point of view you need to do the following:

1. State the main contention of your argument.

    Example: In this story, the writer believes that Pocahontas is a heroine for saving John Smith and preventing the Indians from driving out or killing the explorers. The writer believes that the explorers have a right to conquer the Indians and settle the New World.

2. Make several *claims* to support the main contention of your argument. A claim is a statement that you believe to be true in your analysis of the situation. Your argument may have any number of claims. I will only illustrate two on this guide.

    Claim #1: The writer believes that the Europeans are more civilized than the Indians, and therefore should conquer them.
    Claim #2: The writer believes that the Europeans believe in Christianity, and therefore have a more enlightened way of life.

3. Provide *evidence* to support each one of your claims, usually in the form of examples.

    Claim #1, Evidence #1: The writer describes the Indians as "savages."
    Claim #1, Evidence #2: The writer refers to the Europeans as having more advanced technology by saying that their guns were superior to the Indians' bow and arrow.
    Claim #2, Evidence #1: The writer describes the Indians as "heathens."
    Claim #2, Evidence #2: The writer said that Pocahontas would be rewarded by God for saving John Smith.

4. Provide a *warrant* that explains why each piece of evidence supports the claim it illustrates.

    Claim #1, Evidence #1, Warrant: The writer refers to Indians as "savages" because they don't wear European clothing, they don't live in houses, and they don't have stores to buy food from. They

Students apply a wide range of strategies to comprehend, interpret, evaluate, and appreciate texts. They draw on their prior experience, their interactions with other readers and writers, their knowledge of word meaning and other texts, their word identification strategies, and their understanding of textual features (e.g., sound-letter correspondence, sentence structure, context, graphics).

Students employ a wide range of strategies as they write and use different writing process elements appropriately to communicate with different audiences for a variety of purposes.

live in the woods with animals and therefore are not civilized, and will benefit from being conquered by the European explorers.

Claim #1, Evidence #2, Warrant: The writer describes the ways in which an explorer can kill an Indian easily with a gun, while the Indians must sneak around to be effective with a bow and arrow. Guns are therefore a superior weapon and represent the more advanced European society.

Claim #2, Evidence #1, Warrant: The description of the Indians as "heathens" means that they believe in primitive religions and therefore are not as advanced as Christians.

Claim #2, Evidence #2, Warrant: The writer believes that God will reward Pocahontas for saving the English explorer John Smith from the Indians, and therefore believes that the Christian God is more powerful and better than the Indian gods.

5. You should finally anticipate your opponent's response to your argument, and explain why it is wrong.

Example: Some people might believe that the Europeans are wrong to come to America and conquer the people who lived there and make them change their way of life. These people are wrong because advanced societies have always conquered less advanced societies, and the Europeans were only spreading their own advanced ways to the uncivilized people of the New World. To make an omelet, you have to break a few eggshells.

Ms. Watson reviewed these traits with the class. To help them with generating information for an argument, she led the class in an analysis of a second narrative, this one embodying a Native American perspective to provide a balance for the narrative analyzed on the guide she had passed out. Through this process she helped the students to see how to make claims, find evidence, provide warrants, and rebut opposing arguments.

Students were then given class time to begin their arguments on the perspective taken by the writer of a published Pocahontas narrative. They were allowed to use notes from their discussions and to consult with other group members on the content of their arguments provided that they did so without disturbing other writers at work. They were given two days of class time plus time out of class, and then brought their papers in for small-group peer response. For the first draft of his paper, Jabari wrote the following analysis of Disney's *Pocahontas*:

Disney's *Pocahontas*

Most people think the Disney movie *Pocahontas* is very P.C. I think it's sort of P.C. but not completely. For the most part you get the story from the Indians point of view. Mainly, the white settlers are nice but stupid people but they're led by a pretty evil and greedy guy. On the other hand just about all of the Indians are good.

The leader of the explorers was a really ugly guy named Ratcliffe. He even had an ugly dog. Ratcliffe was only interested in getting rich. He came to America to find gold, and that's it. He liked John Smith mainly because John Smith was a good Indian fighter. Because he was so evil and ugly and was the leader of the settlers, I think the story is told from the Indians' point of view.

Also, the Indians are good people. They believe in family values, even though Powhatan wants Pocahontas to marry Kocoum and she doesn't want to. But Pocahontas loves her father, and the story calls her "his beloved daughter." Powhatan is not ugly and he seems very wise. Since the Indians are shown as one big loving family, the story seems to be about them.

The Indians also really love Nature. When Pocahontas doesn't know what to do, she goes and talks to a tree. She tells John Smith that his people are greedy and don't respect Nature. John Smith at first thought that the Indians were primitive. Pocahontas got pretty mad and John Smith completely changed. Because John Smith changed to be more like Pocahontas, I'd say the story is more from her point of view than his.

Some people might think this story is told from the white people's point of view. John Smith is a real hunk and kind of a hero, so people might think the story's about him. The Indians try to kill John Smith without realizing he's innocent, and he only survives because Pocahontas saves him. And aside from Ratcliffe, the settlers aren't so bad. Also, the way the story's told all of the Indians speak English. But Pocahontas is beautiful, which evens things out. And she's the real hero because she saves him. Even though the settlers turn out OK they actually end up seeming stupid because they've followed this evil guy for so long without realizing he's evil, and finally see things the Indians' way.

So I think the story's told from the Indians' point of view. Mostly this is a love story about people from different backgrounds. But because the story makes the greedy people look bad at the end and because the Indians' natural way of life looks better, I'd say that the story is about the Indians.

Jabari brought his paper to class and got with his group. Ms. Watson asked the students to read one another's papers and evaluate the strength of the claims, the appropriateness of the examples, the clarity of the warrants, and the persuasiveness of the rebuttal of opposing positions. She also asked them to consider other factors: What aspects of the student's writing might interfere with the argument's persuasiveness? Students considered whether improper language use, incorrect punctuation and spelling, and other factors would make the writer less persuasive, and offered suggestions on how to improve the appearance of the argument so it would be taken more seriously.

In looking at Jabari's paper the students attended to the areas that Ms. Watson had asked them to focus on. After reading his paper they made several suggestions:

Michael: Well Jabari this is pretty good. You covered most of the stuff we talked about before.

Jabari: Thanks.

Imelda: Jabari, I think you could do better with these examples.

Jabari: What do you mean?

Imelda: Well, like right here you say that Ratcliffe and his dog are ugly. I think you could quote from the book and use the words the author used. You know, say, where is it in the story. . . here it is, say something like, "Ratcliffe was ugly and was called 'ruthless and ambitious' and 'haughty' and his ugly dog was 'snooty and spoiled,'" something like that.

Michael: Yeah, that's good, that shows what a jerk he was.

> Students read a wide range of literature from many periods in many genres to build an understanding of the many dimensions (e.g., philosophical, ethical, aesthetic) of human experience.

> Students apply a wide range of strategies to comprehend, interpret, evaluate, and appreciate texts. They draw on their prior experience, their interactions with other readers and writers, their knowledge of word meaning and other texts, their word identification strategies, and their understanding of textual features (e.g., sound-letter correspondence, sentence structure, context, graphics).

> Students adjust their use of spoken, written, and visual language (e.g., conventions, style, vocabulary) to communicate effectively with a variety of audiences and for different purposes.

> Students use spoken, written, and visual language to accomplish their own purposes (e.g., for learning, enjoyment, persuasion, and the exchange of information).

Jabari: OK, let me write that down. Anything else?

Luis: Maybe you could add other quotes at other times in the paper.

The students continued to evaluate Jabari's paper in this manner and then proceeded to critique the papers of the other students according to the same criteria. When they were done, they had some class time remaining and began working on their revisions.

Students were then given several days to revise their essays and turn them in to Ms. Watson. To encourage their use of the school's computer lab, she allowed one extra day for students who turned in papers typed on a word processor. For evaluation criteria she used the same attributes that students had considered in their small-group response to one another's essays and stressed in the handout: the manner in which the claims supported the main contention of the argument; the appropriateness of the examples in supporting the claims, as indicated by the warrants; and the persuasiveness of the rebuttal to opposing arguments. She also took into consideration her students' recommendations that papers should be relatively free of errors in grammar, mechanics, and usage in order to be persuasive. She required students to turn in all drafts of their work: any notes they'd taken during the small-group discussion, their first draft including marginal comments made by their peer-response group, any subsequent drafts, and the final product. From this set of drafts she could trace the extent to which students were developing their ideas and monitoring their presentation through the process of composing.

Jabari revised his essay into the following final draft:

Review of Disney's *Pocahontas: The Book*

Everybody thinks that the Disney movie *Pocahontas* is very P.C. I read the book that they made about the movie, and I think it's sort of P.C., but not completely. For the most part you get the story from the Indians' point of view. Mainly, the white settlers are nice but stupid people but they're led by a pretty evil and greedy guy. On the other hand just about all of the Indians are good. I'll explain why.

The leader of the *Susan Constant* was a really ugly guy named John Ratcliffe. The story called him "ruthless and ambitious" and "haughty" and he even had an ugly dog who was called "snooty and spoiled." John Ratcliffe was only interested in getting rich. He came to the New World to find gold, and didn't even care about the king and queen of England who'd sent him, even though he pretended to. He liked John Smith mainly because John Smith was a good Indian fighter. Because he was so evil and ugly and was the leader of the settlers, I think the story is told from the Indians' point of view more than the settlers' point of view.

Also, the Indians are shown to be very good people. They believe in family values, even though Powhatan wants Pocahontas to marry a pretty boring guy named Kocoum and she doesn't want to. Kocoum gets killed later on so she doesn't have to go through with it. But Pocahontas loves her father, and the story calls her "his beloved daughter." Powhatan is not ugly, he's usually smiling until the settlers kill Kocoum. And he seems very wise, compared to the greedy John Ratcliffe. Since the Indians are shown as one big loving family, the story seems to be told from their point of view.

The Indians also really love Nature. When Pocahontas doesn't know what to do, she goes and talks to a tree. She also has a favorite place to go, which is on a cliff where she can see a beautiful waterfall. She tells John Smith that his people are greedy and don't respect Nature, and he changes from being an Indian fighter to being an Indian lover. John Smith at first thought that the Indians were primitive. He told Pocahontas, "There's so much we can teach you. We've improved the lives of savages all over the world." Pocahontas got pretty mad and showed John Smith the wonders of Nature and he completely changed. Because John Smith changed to be more like Pocahontas, I'd say the story is more from her point of view than his.

Some people might think this story is told from the white people's point of view. John Smith is handsome with long blond hair, and he's kind of a hero, so people might think the story's about him. The Indians try to kill John Smith without realizing he's innocent, and he only survives because Pocahontas saves him. And aside from Ratcliffe, the settlers aren't so bad, especially at the end when they decide that it's wrong to be greedy and lock Ratcliffe up. Also, the way the story's told all of the Indians speak English, which some people might think means that the settlers were superior. But I don't think so. John Smith's handsome, but Pocahontas is beautiful, which evens things out. And she's the real hero because she saves him. Even though the settlers turn out not being so bad at the end, they actually end up seeming kind of stupid because they've followed this evil guy for so long without realizing he's evil, and finally see things the Indians' way. Finally, I think the person who wrote the story made the Indians speak English so most people could understand what they were saying, not because it's a better language.

So I think the story's told from the Indians' point of view. Mostly this is a love story about people from different backgrounds, kind of like *Romeo and Juliet* except they don't die at the end, even though they have to split up. But because the story makes the greedy people look bad at the end and because the Indians' natural way of life looks better, I'd say that the Indians are the ones who win this time.

Following this introduction, Ms. Watson told the students that they would spend the next three weeks of class time writing their families' immigration stories. She talked with them about what they might learn through researching their family histories. She started by talking about some things she might like to learn about her own family's experiences with immigration, and said that she would try to find out about her own history as they were researching theirs. Ms. Watson knew that her ancestry was English, Norwegian, Swedish, and Portuguese, but wasn't entirely certain when each branch of the family had left Europe or why her ancestors had left their homelands. She thought it would be interesting to learn about what had motivated them to leave: economics, discrimination, adventure, religion, or something else.

She then asked students what they would like to learn about their family histories. Some said they wanted to talk to their grandparents to understand the experience of leaving a homeland and coming to live in a foreign place. Others wanted to understand whether their ancestors had wanted to assimilate into American culture or preserve their old ways. Others wanted to learn about the journey itself: What was it like to travel on a boat across an ocean, or to cross a border to live in a foreign land, leaving possessions and customs behind? Some African American students wondered if there were differences between people who chose to emigrate, and people who were forced to leave a homeland to become a free person's property. A student who had both Native American and European blood wondered how the different sides of her family viewed the consequences of the European settlement of the continent.

Students conduct research on issues and interests by generating ideas and questions, and by posing problems. They gather, evaluate, and synthesize data from a variety of sources (e.g., print and nonprint texts, artifacts, people) to communicate their discoveries in ways that suit their purpose and audience.

After discussing possible motivations for conducting research on family experiences with immigration, Ms. Watson told the students that to help them produce their stories she was going to alter the way in which she set up the classroom. Her overriding goal was to have students develop personal perspectives on immigration, and she anticipated that each history would be different, not only in content but in medium and format. She therefore wanted to make the classroom structure informal so as to allow students freedom in the choices they made. She had attended the state NCTE affiliate conference the previous year and had talked to teachers who used "writing workshops" in which students used class time to develop writing of their choice, and saw an opportunity to adapt the idea to her "Coming to America" unit. Because she encouraged students to create both written and multimedia productions, she thought of it more as a "composing workshop" than as a writing workshop.

She raised the workshop idea with her students and they approved of it. Once they agreed to use this format, she said that for the next few weeks they would be able to make decisions about how to spend their class time, as long as they used it productively. Ms. Watson decided to consult the students about how to set up the parameters of the workshop to guide their classroom production. She posed the question one day in class: "We are going to spend class time this marking period writing personal immigration histories. To do so, we will change the way we use the classroom so that you can make choices about how you spend your time. At times you will stay here and work; at times you may go to another part of the building to work. In order for us to stay with this arrangement, we need to set up some rules to govern our activities. What guidelines can you suggest that will help us use our time productively?" She suggested that the class think of rules that structure performance in a variety of contexts: rules or laws that people follow in society, in school, at work, in games, in other areas of social life. What, she asked, is the purpose of a law? Is there one set of laws that guides all behavior, or does the context matter? What are the consequences of breaking rules? What types of guidelines would best govern their efforts to use class time productively to create family immigration stories?

The students raised a variety of issues. Were rules helpful to people in conducting themselves, or did they overregulate people's freedom? Did rules encourage people to respect one another, or only provide them with incentives for misconduct? Why was the same crime, such as theft, punished one way in Saudi Arabia and another in the United States? Is school important enough to care whether or not rules are followed? Did there need to be an umpire for deciding who follows the rules in the classroom? What is the purpose of school rules?

After a lengthy discussion the class agreed on a small set of rules to govern their behavior. The fundamental rule that they identified was the need to spend class time on their projects. If they signed out to go to the library and went somewhere else instead, this was a violation of their agreement to follow the rules, and would place the integrity of the whole class in jeopardy. The class voted that any students who signed out for one area and instead went elsewhere had to stay after school with Ms. Watson for one hour as she called parents, graded papers, filled out student reports, and attended to the other school business that she normally took care of after school. This punishment was the worst the class could think of—students who stayed after school missed their jobs and threatened their employment. Within class, students needed to work productively or face the same consequences; students were welcome to collaborate on their work, but could not distract others or do nothing.

Taking into consideration the interests students had expressed in conducting personal research on immigration, Ms. Watson then posed the specific question that would guide their research, which she distributed in a handout:

> You have access to many sources of information about your family's role in American immigration, including people in the community, books, films, and information from the Internet. Different people have different perspectives on immigration depending on their experiences. Your job is to develop some type of presentation on your family's experiences with immigration to the American continent. You may collect information from any sources available to you for your project. Some possible questions to consider are: If your family immigrated to America, why did they leave their former country? Were the reasons religious, economic, ethnic, legal, or something else? Did they leave voluntarily or were they forced to leave? What did America offer them that they lacked before? What did America lack that they had before? Ultimately, how do you view your position as an American from the standpoint of your family's immigration story?
>
> If your ancestors were natives of this continent, how do you view the changes brought about by the immigration of other people to this land? How has your family experienced the arrival of people from other nations? How do you view the development of the United States of America on this continent? What have been the consequences to you?
>
> For your project you may develop any mode of presentation that you choose. You may write a research paper the way students usually do in school. You may prepare a documentary film such as the ones you've seen on television. You may prepare a hypertext presentation on a computer. You may produce a "docudrama" which is an imaginative presentation of history. You may write an opera. Or you can develop a presentation that combines these forms, or others of your choice.

With these guidelines established, Ms. Watson and the students set up the classroom so that it would facilitate their work. With so many students holding after-school jobs, few could meet her unit goals unless substantial class time was devoted to work on their projects. In addition, she wanted to be available for students to consult with her as their work progressed. To make the classroom as conducive as possible to the development of student projects, Ms. Watson transformed it into a resource center that was writing center, museum, think tank, studio, gallery, and library all rolled into one. One corner of the room included books and other resources that students could check out to use for their projects. Concerned that the choices available in the American literature anthology provided too narrow a view of the explorers and native people of the continent, she first sought to include more varied perspectives on the colonial period. The school library had recently acquired the video series *How the West Was Lost* that presented the story of European settlement from a Native American perspective, and she received permission to move this collection to her classroom for the duration of the unit. Along with this videotape she checked out a TV with VCR and headphones so that students could watch parts of the series in class. In addition, she prepared a list of other video productions for students to draw on to consider the history of the continent from a variety of perspectives. This list included not just documentaries, but fictional and autobiographical films that dealt with immigration such as *The Godfather, Part II* and the *Roots* series. Throughout the unit students were encouraged to add to this list both titles and summaries and reviews of movies they had seen. Students interested in a film could consult the set of reviews to help make a decision on whether or not to see it. Two students who had seen *The Godfather, Part II* wrote conflicting reviews of the film:

Review of *The Godfather, Part II*

I think this movie stinks. My family is Italian and everyone thinks we're gangsters. The reason is that they've seen movies like *The Godfather Part II* where an Italian immigrant comes to America and can't find a job and so starts killing people for the Mafia and stealing things. There probably are real people like that, but all this movie does is create stereotypes. Every Italian in the movie is a gangster. But I live in the Italian part of the city and everybody I know has a normal job. Nobody I know kills people or runs a protection racket or anything like that. You might like this movie because it's exciting, but don't believe that all Italians are like the Corleones.

Review of *The Godfather, Part II*

This is a great movie that everyone ought to see. It gives a real feeling of what it was like to be in New York City a long time ago. And Robert DiNiro is a great actor in the movie, and so is Marlon Brando and Al Pacino. I read Chuck's review and I disagree. All of these actors are Italian and so is Mario Puzo who wrote the book and so is the director who made it, so I don't think the Italians are being stereotyped since they're the ones who made the movie. The Mafia is real and there's one right here in this city, so I think it's a good way to learn about what happened to Italians who came to America back then. And it's a really exciting movie too. Even though there's a lot of blood and killing, it's still very educational and very entertaining. I recommend that you see it so you can make up your own mind.

Students could consult these reviews to decide whether to watch the videos to help them with their projects or simply to see them for entertainment.

The in-class library also included books and magazines that students could check out. These books concerned immigration stories from a variety of nations and cultures, including historical narratives and fiction. Again, students were encouraged to add titles to this list and provide summaries and reviews of those they'd read. Ms. Watson required students to complete a minimum number of compositions of their choice to be submitted at the end of the unit in a portfolio.

> Students use spoken, written, and visual language to accomplish their own purposes (e.g., for learning, enjoyment, persuasion, and the exchange of information).

> Students develop an understanding of and respect for diversity in language use, patterns, and dialects across cultures, ethnic groups, geographic regions, and social roles.

I will challenge the prevalent belief in "coverage," that the course of study which spreads over many areas is necessarily better than a more modest one. . . . My basic conclusion is contained in the aphorism "Less is more." I believe that the qualities of mind that should be the goal of high school need time to grow and that they develop best when engaging in a few, important ideas, deeply. Information is plentiful, cheap; learning how to use it is often stressful and absolutely requires a form of personal coaching of each student by a teacher that is neither possible in many schools today nor recognized as an important process.

Theodore R. Sizer, *Horace's Compromise*, p. 89.

Ms. Watson wanted students to draw on a variety of resources. She wanted to make sure that their resources included the traditional classics from the course anthology. She also wanted students to draw on other sources from either the classroom library or elsewhere. She therefore required all students to keep a journal in response to all the reading they did to inform their research, and required that they show evidence of reading at least four selections from the anthology and four from other sources. Their log could include any response they had to the selections, but needed to indicate clearly that they had read them and related them to their research.

Ms. Watson realized that she herself could not sufficiently provide the resources for the projects that she envisioned her students producing. The classroom resources, while helpful in getting students started, would be insufficient for them to complete their projects. In order for them to produce a quality effort they needed to draw on additional outside resources that she would recommend to them. In addition, at the beginning of the unit she sent a note home to each parent and guardian explaining the unit and asking for volunteers to come to the class to share their stories with the students. She also contacted a history professor at one of the city colleges who specialized in the colonial period and had her to visit the class for a brief lecture and an extended question and answer period.

Traditionally, students had produced research papers by using index cards for notes, writing a rough draft, typing it, and then turning it in. Ms. Watson felt that some recent developments in her community could help her students produce research reports that took advantage of some new technologies that were available. Two types of technology in particular could, she felt, both increase students' interest in the project and provide them with technological literacy that would help them better succeed in the world economy of the future.

The first of these was the Internet. The city public library had recently provided an Internet connection that was available to all citizens, including her students. Ms. Watson took them on a field trip to the city library, where the librarian's technical assistant oriented them to the Internet, provided them with access addresses, and taught them how to use the software to "surf" the Internet in search of information that would help their research efforts. The students learned how to access remote libraries, newspapers, museums, archives, and other sources of information. They also discovered online discussion groups that ended up benefitting some. One student came across a network that provided a forum for holocaust survivors to stay in touch, and received permission to use some of their Internet comments and stories as part of his report on the immigration of German Jews in the 1930s and 1940s, the period when his grandparents had migrated.

The second technology students learned to use was computer-based hypermedia. The school's business department had recently installed a new computer lab, and Ms. Watson developed a partnership that allowed her students access to the lab during periods when business students were not using it. In preparing their reports students had the option of presenting them as hypertext productions; instead of presenting their reports in the conventional linear format, their presentation would begin with an opening orientation page that would allow a user to click on specific topics and explore available information.

Other students conducted more primary research. With their extended families living in the neighborhood, many students could simply go down the block to talk to older relatives and community members about their reasons for immi-

— Students read a wide range of print and nonprint texts to build an understanding of texts, of themselves, and of the cultures of the United States and the world; to acquire new information; to respond to the needs and demands of society and the workplace; and for personal fulfillment. Among these texts are fiction and nonfiction, classic and contemporary works.

— Students use a variety of technological and informational resources (e.g., libraries, databases, computer networks, video) to gather and synthesize information and to create and communicate knowledge.

grating and the stories of their experiences. Ms. Watson helped students learn how to conduct interviews by sharing with them some of her own methods for researching her own history. She tape-recorded a phone conversation with an older relative, played it for the class, and also gave them a copy of the questions she'd asked. She invited her aunt to visit the class and interviewed her before them, showing students how to tape-record an interview, take notes, and pose questions.

Ms. Watson also thought that students could learn something from their after-school work that could inform their research. Often their work in local businesses and factories brought them into contact with older members of the community who had come from "the old country" or who were connected to bygone generations. Ms. Watson encouraged students to use their coworkers as resources for their research.

For their own research students were encouraged to audiotape conversations and transcribe them for inclusion in the text of their reports. Students with access to videocameras could also videotape older family members to get their stories and artifacts on film. Students could conduct the interviews in both English and, if desired, their family's native tongue. If they chose, students could scan the voices and images from their primary-source research onto hypercards and include them in hypermedia productions. For some students music, food, and other cultural practices were central to their stories. They were encouraged to include examples of the ways in which such practices were involved in resettlement.

As noted, Ms. Watson made a link with the school's business department to allow her students access to advanced computer technology. In addition, she turned to other departments in the school for resources her students could use to their advantage. In directing the school's plays she had become friends with the art teacher, who helped design the sets. The art teacher visited class one day with samples from her slide collection and agreed to lend students images that they could incorporate into their productions. Ms. Watson's hall duty was scheduled near the history department chair's office, and she informed her of the unit so that students could more explicitly apply lessons from one class to the other. One of the biology teachers was a personal friend of Ms. Watson's and came to class to talk about how conditions create the famines that accounted for the immigration of the Irish and other groups to America.

Ms. Watson believed that she could not single-handedly oversee each student's progress towards the completion of such complex productions. She also knew that students would benefit from getting a variety of viewpoints in developing their work. She therefore enlisted the support of parents and other family members, other teachers, librarians, and the extended human resources provided through the Internet to help her students develop their projects. She also encouraged students to work together on their projects; students of similar backgrounds could collaborate on their productions, and they were always allowed to consult with one another and review each other's work as they proceeded. The social organization of the classroom encouraged students to talk to one another frequently during their research efforts and to provide one another with information about useful resources. Ms. Watson additionally worked with students during the process of their research, holding formal conferences with individuals and groups every other week and providing additional consultation as requested by students.

Ms. Watson found that with such a multilayered structure to the class, she needed to be highly organized in order for the unit to be successful. Students who went to the library, business computing lab, or other location needed to sign out, and spent an afternoon after school with Ms. Watson if they went elsewhere, as agreed upon by the class. She conducted and recorded a brief daily survey of each student's progress which contributed to student accountability. These records also helped her account for student productivity when parents or colleagues inquired about the unconventional instruction taking place in her class. She arranged the physical structure of the classroom to facilitate productivity, providing carrels, conference areas, tables, and an area to store student folders. She also kept a public chart on the class bulletin board where students kept a record of their reading, which other students could consult to inform their own reading choices. Each student additionally kept an "Organizer" for storing records of writing conferences, research notes, and other types of information that were used for both student resources and parent-teacher conferences. On Fridays the students gave a progress report for their week's activities and a plan for what they hoped to accomplish the next week.

One of Ms. Watson's greatest concerns was that by focusing on individual heritages she would encourage separation along racial and ethnic lines. Students in her school were already segregated enough, she felt, and she feared that by encouraging them to define themselves according to their differences, she could deepen some of the schisms that already existed. As the unit developed, she realized that it would only succeed if it served to create a classroom community that helped students understand the complex fabric of American society. The unit "Coming to America" thus needed to end in an exploration of the question: Considering all the differences among American citizens, what does it mean to be a member of American society today?

In order to answer this question, each student needed to become acquainted with one another's stories. Ms. Watson realized that the class had in part reached this goal through a social environment in which the students conducted their research, allowing them to follow one another's stories as they were being constructed. Yet since students tended to socialize with friends rather than those with whom they had differences, she was concerned that the greatest social chasms threatened to remain open. Ms. Watson decided that a more public presentation of the productions was necessary in order for students to learn about one another and

Students develop an understanding of and respect for diversity in language use, patterns, and dialects across cultures, ethnic groups, geographic regions, and social roles.

develop a sense of kinship as a community. The class did not have time for twenty-eight individual presentations, so she asked students to form groups of people with similar backgrounds and create a presentation on the experiences of their ethnic groups in the context of American immigration. No one student presented the whole of his or her research, but each student's story became part of the class's understanding of American history. Students were provided two days of preparation time, and then each group could take up to one class period for its presentation. They were encouraged to supplement their report with food, photographs, artwork, and other cultural tools and artifacts central to their group's history.

In presenting their research, many students alluded to their families' interest in their projects. In Ms. Watson's conferences she learned that family members who were consulted on the project often requested copies of the finished product, and that students often shared their findings at the dinner table and other family gatherings. The research thus reached an important audience beyond the classroom.

Ms. Watson suggested that the students set aside an evening where they set up their projects and display them for interested community members. Many students objected, however, saying that they could not miss work, or that their older relatives did not like to go into the school neighborhood at night. They suggested instead that they display their projects in the school library, where other students could see them and where relatives could come by during the day. Ms. Watson proposed this idea to the librarian, who agreed to set aside space for any students who wanted to display their projects.

Following these presentations, Ms. Watson organized the class into heterogeneous groups of four to five students and gave them the question: Considering all the differences among American citizens, what does it mean to be a member of American society today? The groups discussed this question, then met together as a class to explore it further.

To follow up this discussion, as a final project for the unit students contrasted their own "Coming to America" history with that of someone whose experience was significantly different. Ms. Watson hoped that in so doing students would consider the perspective of someone else and gain a broader understanding of the different views of America and a better understanding of how to resolve these differences. Students could choose to contrast themselves with either another student from the class, or with someone whose experiences they encountered through their reading or viewing. If they chose a classmate for comparison, they needed to get the student's permission first, in order to protect the student from unwelcome personal critiques. In keeping with the open-ended emphasis of the unit as a whole, she gave students a choice of writing a conventional comparison/contrast essay, writing a work of fiction that dramatized two different types of experience, or other medium of their choice. Students produced drafts, worked together in peer-response groups for feedback, and ultimately turned in final copies for grades.

Linda, a mixed-race student officially classified as Native American in school records, produced the following paper based on her interactions during the unit with Mai, the daughter of Vietnamese refugees:

Two Views of America

My experiences as an American are very different from most people's in this class. I am part Cherokee and Osage Indian and also part Irish and

Hungarian. I have many heritages, but my Cherokee ancestors are the ones I think of most when thinking about who I am. Most people don't know it, but we have a very complicated history.

Originally my people lived in what is now called Georgia. After white people came from Europe and took over the eastern part of the country, they decided they didn't want Indians around any more. So they found a place in the middle of the country where only Indians lived and decided to move Eastern Indians out to live there. The path they took out West is called the Trail of Tears because so many people died on the way. They finally ended up in a place called Oklahoma Territory. The word Oklahoma means both Red Earth and Red People.

Indians who already lived in this territory did not want eastern Indians to come out an live on their traditional lands, and so there were many wars between the original plains Indians and the ones from the east. The Osage were natives to the land, and battled the Cherokee, so my ancestors were once at war. The U.S. Army was supposed to keep the peace, which just added one more group to the fight. Some of these soldiers were Irish, which was one more group of my ancestors who fought against each other.

Cherokee Indians took to white people's ways very easily. They developed a written language and became plantation farmers. It's hard for me to believe it now, but about 150 years ago my ancestors owned black slaves on their plantation. They fought on the side of the South during the civil war. After the war they lost their land. Eventually my people ended up here, and married white people and now we live in an apartment, watch TV, go to school, and do other normal American things. But I have a different feeling about America than most people in my class because I still wonder what it would be like to live in the old way.

My life as an American is very different from Mai Nguy's, but in some ways it's the same. Mai's parents came here from Viet Nam in the seventies when they were teenagers. In Viet Nam everything was a mess. There was a civil war, and America and other countries tried to help out each side. When Mai's people lost, her parents and many others from their village got on rafts and headed out to sea. After many stops, they ended up in America. So they were like us because they had to leave their home and move to a place far away, and they didn't have any choice about whether or not to move. They were different in that my people were told where they had to live, and Mai's people just got on boats hoping they'd find some place that would take them. And my people were ordered to leave by outsiders, while she had to leave because her own people were trying to kill her.

Mai's parents now speak English OK, even though when they came and talked to our class I had trouble understanding them. But Mai talks just like us and will probably end up being a normal American just the way I am, sort of. We're different because she really feels that America is a much better place for her to live in than her old home because there are no wars to worry about. I still feel kind of mad that my people had to change their lifestyle and leave their home.

The unit that Daphne Watson taught on "Coming to America" ended up going well beyond the three-week time period she'd initially planned. However, once it was under way she could not interrupt students' progress on their research and consideration of the unit's concepts. The unit's length caused her to reconsider how to plan her implementation of the curriculum for the remainder of the first semester. Her value on the process of her students' learning, however, justified the compromise in terms of coverage, even if it created some stress for her. Some of her students were concerned that they were "getting behind" other classes, and some of her colleagues clearly did not approve of what they felt was her cavalier approach to the curriculum, but Ms. Watson felt vindicated by the performance of her students on their projects.

She also found that the "Coming to America" unit helped set the stage for the remainder of the year's learning, thus calling into question the criticism that she had sacrificed a portion of the curriculum to accommodate the students' work on their projects. She saw the curriculum as involving a flow of ideas, rather than being partitioned into sections, and so saw their work on their projects as part of a larger process of considering the issues raised in American literature. The class's attention to historical perspectives provided the basis for a year-long critique of narrative point of view, both in fiction and nonfiction prose. Students looked at the narrators in *The Red Badge of Courage, The Scarlet Letter,* and other stories and imagined how the story could be told by other characters. At times the students took episodes from the literature and rewrote them, narrating the same action from other characters' perspectives. In addition, her instruction in argumentation enabled her to ask her students to write increasingly sophisticated arguments, and students became adept at persuading other people of their views in both class discussions and in writing.

Finally, the classroom structure she adopted for the research workshop affected the class for the rest of the year. The students often worked in social configurations, using the class as a resource center to inform their inquiries. While Ms. Watson did not abandon convention altogether, she often returned to the class's informal arrangement, with students frequently working collaboratively on projects, in small-group discussions and in pairs. Her use of portfolio principles continued as she gave students options on choosing compositions to develop into polished pieces, and she urged them to reflect on their composing processes in writing, discussion, and other formats. The unit, therefore, provided the intellectual and procedural foundation for the students' learning for the rest of the year.

The main tension that Ms. Watson experienced through her restructuring of the classroom to facilitate learning processes was in terms of the conflict that developed in covering the prescribed curriculum. Lincoln High School was a curriculum-driven place, and Ms. Watson had covered far less of the American literature anthology than did her colleagues. This change in priorities concerned some of her students, who worried that they were missing out on something important by not reading all of the anthology selections. This regard for covering the curriculum was also shared by some parents who visited class on Parents' Night and as guest speakers for the class. On the other hand, Ms. Watson had far more parental contact, for better or worse, during this unit than at any other time during her brief career.

Daphne Watson also had to defend herself to her department chair against the complaints of some colleagues who clearly disapproved of her innovations. Her justification for her methods came through the work of her students, and the records she kept of their progress. While no longer a comfortable fit with

Students apply a wide range of strategies to comprehend, interpret, evaluate, and appreciate texts. They draw on their prior experience, their interactions with other readers and writers, their knowledge of word meaning and other texts, their word identification strategies, and their understanding of textual features (e.g., sound-letter correspondence, sentence structure, context, graphics).

the conventional ways of teaching practiced in her department and throughout her school, her teaching was, she felt, more compatible with her students' learning needs.

Standards in Practice

Students in Ms. Watson's class engage with a wide range of print and nonprint texts to explore their own personal histories, the histories of their classmates, and the histories of other Americans that are represented in book, film, and personal narrative. Their personal family histories provide the basis for their understanding of the development of society on the North American continent, and their development of their research projects engages them in the gathering, evaluation, and synthesis of data from many sources. Additionally, their research takes place over many weeks, and thus engages them in a process of composition through which they must consider the conventions of the genre in which they are working and the needs of the audience with whom they hope to communicate. Through their exposure to the immigration experiences of people from many backgrounds, they need to consider the moral and aesthetic dimensions of the establishment of the United States and the impact of the development of this society on people representing groups with different degrees of power and advantage. Students use technology to gather and synthesize information and communicate with others. In many cases, they account for linguistic diversity and second language acquisition through their exploration of immigrant groups' experiences. Through their personal explorations of their family histories, and through their exposure to the stories of other class members, they participate in a variety of literacy communities and develop personal goals for conducting research in the school setting.

Resources

Teaching ESL Students

Books

Benesch, S. (Ed.). (1990). *ESL in America: Myths and possibilities.* Portsmouth, NH: Boynton/Cook Publishers.

Brumfit, C. (1984). *Communicative methodology in language teaching: The roles of fluency and accuracy.* New York: Cambridge University Press.

Edelsky, C. (1986). *Writing in a bilingual program: Había una vez.* Norwood, NJ: Ablex Publishing Corp.

Freeman, D. E., & Freeman, Y. S. (1994). *Between worlds: Access to second language acquisition.* Portsmouth, NH: Heinemann.

Johnson, D. M., & Roen, D. H. (Eds.). (1989). *Richness in writing: Empowering ESL students*. New York: Longman.

Kroll, B. (Ed.). (1990). *Second language writing: Research insights for the classroom*. New York: Cambridge University Press.

Leki, I. (1992). *Understanding ESL writers: A guide for teachers*. Portsmouth, NH: Boynton/Cook Publishers.

Moskowitz, G. (1978). *Caring and sharing in the foreign language class*. Rowley, MA: Newbury House.

Murray, D. E. (Ed.). (1992). *Diversity as resource*. Alexandria, VA: Teachers of English to Speakers of Other Languages, Inc.

Nelson, M. W. (1991). *At the point of need: Teaching basic and ESL writers*. Portsmouth, NH: Boynton/Cook Publishers.

Nuttall, C. (1982). *Teaching reading skills in a foreign language*. London: Educational Books.

Peyton, J. K., & Reed, L. (1990). *Dialogue journal writing w/nonnative English speakers: A handbook for teachers*. Alexandria, VA: Teachers of English to Speakers of Other Languages, Inc.

Purves, A. C. (Ed.). (1988). *Writing across languages and cultures: Issues in contrastive rhetoric*. Newbury Park, CA: Sage Publications.

Raimes, A. (1992). *Exploring through writing: A process approach to ESL composition* (2nd ed.). New York: St. Martin's Press.

Reid, J. M. (1993). *Teaching ESL writing*. Englewood Cliffs, NJ: Regents/Prentice-Hall.

Richards, J. C., & Rodgers, T. S. (1986). *Approaches and methods in language teaching: A description and analysis*. New York: Cambridge University Press.

Rigg, P., & Allen, V. G. (Eds.). (1989). *When they don't all speak English: Integrating the ESL student into the regular classroom*. Urbana, IL: National Council of Teachers of English.

Rigg, P., & Enright, D. S. (Eds.). (1986). *Children and ESL: Integrating perspectives*. Washington, D.C.: Teachers of English to Speakers of Other Languages, Inc.

Rodby, J. (1992). *Appropriating literacy: Writing and reading English as a second language*. Portsmouth, NH: Boynton/Cook Publishers.

Spangenberg-Urbschat, K., & Pritchard, R. (Eds.). (1994). *Kids come in all languages*. Newark, DE: International Reading Association.

Trueba, H., Guthrie, G., & Au, K. (Eds.). *Culture and the bilingual classroom: Studies in classroom ethnography*. Rowley, MA: Newbury House Publishers.

Warschauer, M. (1995). *E-mail for English teaching*. Alexandria, VA: Teachers of English to Speakers of Other Languages, Inc.

Journals

ELT Journal

English Plus: Issues in Bilingual Education, Sage Publications

Journal of Second Language Writing, Ablex Publishing Corporation

Teaching English as a Second or Foreign Language: An Electronic Journal, to subscribe, type: listserv@cmsa.berkeley.edu

TESOL Journal, Teachers of English to Speakers of Other Languages, Inc.

TESOL Quarterly, Teachers of English to Speakers of Other Languages, Inc.

TESL Canada Journal, Faculty of Education, McGill University, Montreal, Quebec

TESL Talk, Newcomers Service Branch, Toronto, Ontario

Organizations and Committees

NCTE English as a Second Language Assembly

Teachers of English to Speakers of Other Languages, Inc., 1600 Cameron St., Suite 300, Alexandria, VA 22314-2751

E-mail Network

TESL-L@cunyvm.cuny.edu

Versions of the Pocahontas Tale

Books

Adams, P. (1987). *The story of Pocahontas, Indian princess.* New York: Dell Publishing Company.

Benjamin, A. (1992). *Young Pocahontas: Indian princess.* Mahwah, NJ: Troll Associates.

Bulla, C. R. (1971). *Pocahontas and the strangers.* New York: Crowell.

d'Aulaire, I., & d'Aulaire, E. (1946). *Pocahontas.* Garden City, NY: Doubleday.

Disney's Pocahontas. (1995). United States of America: Mouse Works.

Dougherty, K. (1995). *The legend of Pocahontas.* New York: Children's Classics.

Faber, D. (1963). *The life of Pocahontas.* Englewood Cliffs, NJ: Prentice-Hall.

Fritz, J. (1983). *The double life of Pocahontas.* New York: Putnam.

Gleiter, J., & Thompson, K. (1985). *Pocahontas.* Milwaukee, WI: Raintree Publishers.

Greene, C. (1988). *Pocahontas: Daughter of a chief.* Chicago: Children's Press.

Jassem, K. (1979). *Pocahontas, girl of Jamestown.* Mahwah, NJ: Troll Associates.

Video

Pocahontas. (1995). Walt Disney Studios.

Scholarship about Pocahontas

Books

Barbour, P. (1970). *Pocahontas and her world: A chronicle of America's first settlement in which is related the story of the Indians and the Englishmen, particularly captain John Smith, captain Samuel Argall, and master John Rolfe.* Boston: Houghton Mifflin.

d'Aulaire, I., & d'Aulaire, E. (1989). *Pocahontas.* New York: Doubleday.

Donnell, S. (1991). *Pocahontas.* New York: Berkeley Books.

Feest, C. F. (1989). *The Powhatan tribes.* New York: Chelsea House Publishers.

Holler, A. (1993). *Pocahontas, Powhatan peacemaker.* New York: Chelsea House Publishers.

Mossiker, F. (1976). *Pocahontas: The life and the legend.* New York: Knopf.

Phillips, L. (1973). *First lady of America: A romanticized biography of Pocahontas.* Richmond, VA: Westover Publishing Company.

Rountree, H. (1990). *Pocahontas's people: The Powhatan Indians of Virginia through four centuries.* Norman, OK: University of Oklahoma Press.

Smith, J. (1970). *Captain John Smith's history of Virginia: A selection.* Indianapolis: Bobbs-Merrill.

Tilton, R. (1994). *Pocahontas: The evolution of an American narrative.* New York: Cambridge University Press.

Woodward, G. S. (1969). *Pocahontas.* Norman, OK: University of Oklahoma Press.

Video

Pocahontas. A&E Biography series.

Teaching Personal Research

Books

Atwell, N. (Ed.). (1990). *Coming to know: Writing to learn in the intermediate grades.* Portsmouth, NH: Heinemann.

Dixon, D. (1993). *Writing your heritage: A sequence of thinking, reading, and writing assignments.* Berkeley, CA: National Writing Project.

Macrorie, K. (1988). *The I-search paper.* Portsmouth, NH: Heinemann.

Rief, L. (1992). *Seeking diversity: Language arts with adolescents.* Portsmouth, NH: Heinemann Educational Books.

Sharan, Y., & Sharan, S. (1992). *Expanding cooperative learning through group investigation.* New York: Teachers College Press.

Ward, G. (1989). *I've got a project on.* Portsmouth, NH: Heinemann.

Weitzman, D. (1975). *My backyard history book.* Boston: Little, Brown.

Wigginton, E. (1975). *Moments: The Foxfire experience.* Nederland, CO: IDEAS.

Wigginton, E. (1985). *Sometimes a shining moment: The Foxfire experience.* Garden City, NY: Anchor Press/Doubleday.

Journal

Hands On: A Journal for Teachers, Foxfire Fund, Rabun Gap, GA 30568

Conducting Workshops

Books and Articles

Atwell, N. (1987). *In the middle: Writing, reading, and learning with adolescents.* Upper Montclair, NJ: Boynton/Cook Publishers.

Calkins, L. M. (1987). *The writing workshop: A world of difference/a guide for staff development.* Portsmouth, NH: Heinemann.

Calkins, L. M. (1991). *Living between the lines.* Portsmouth, NH: Heinemann.

Hartman, D. K., & Hartman, J. A. (1993). Reading across texts: Expanding the role of the reader. *Reading Teacher, 47*(3), 202–211.

Hynds, S. (in press). *Negotiating the brink: Coming to literature and literacy in an urban middle school.* New York: Teachers College Press.

Krogness, M. M. (1995). *Just teach me, Mrs. K: Talking, reading, and writing with resistant adolescent learners.* Portsmouth, NH: Heinemann.

Lensmire, T. (1994). *When children write: Critical re-visions of the writing workshop.* New York: Teachers College Press.

Rief, L. (1992). *Seeking diversity: Language arts with adolescents.* Portsmouth, NH: Heinemann Educational Books.

Romano, T. (1987). *Clearing the way: Working with teenage writers.* Portsmouth, NH: Heinemann.

Videos

A circle of writers: The Peabody High School Writing Workshop. (1993). The Video Difference.

Snake Hill to Spring Bank: A classroom publishing project. (1984). Alexandria, VA: The Associations.

Stories about Immigration

Film

Documentary:
How the West was lost
The way west

Fiction and Autobiography:
Avalon
El Norte
Far and away
The godfather, part II
The immigrants
The Joy Luck Club
Little Odessa
Moscow on the Hudson
My family
Once upon a time in America
Roots

Literature, Biography, and History

Abrahams, R. D., & Szwed, J. F. (Eds.). (1983). *After Africa: Extracts from British travel accounts and journals of the seventeenth, eighteenth, and nineteenth centuries concerning the slaves, their manners, and customs in the British West Indies.* New Haven, CT: Yale University Press.

Acosta, O. Z. (1989). *The autobiography of a brown buffalo.* New York: Vintage Books.

Acosta, O. Z. (1989). *The revolt of the cockroach people.* New York: Vintage Books.

Agnew, B. (1980). *Fort Gibson: Terminal on the Trail of Tears.* Norman, OK: University of Oklahoma Press.

Andryszewski, T. (1994). *Immigration: Newcomers and their impact on the United States.* Brookfield, CT: Millbrook Press.

Aparicio, F. R. (Ed.). (1994). *Latino voices.* Brookfield, CT: Millbrook Press.

Bascom, W. (1972). *Shango in the New World.* Austin, TX: African and Afro-American Institute, University of Texas.

Blassingame, J. W. (Ed.). (1977). *Slave testimony: Two centuries of letters, speeches, interviews, and autobiographies.* Baton Rouge, LA: Louisiana State University Press.

Bode, J. (1989). *New kids on the block: Oral histories of immigrant teens.* New York: Franklin Watts.

Brent, L. (1973). *Incidents in the life of a slave girl.* San Diego: Harcourt.

Bryan, A. (1982). *I'm going to sing: Black American spirituals* (Vol. 2). New York: Atheneum.

Buczek, D. S. (1974). *Immigrant pastor: The life of the Right Reverend Monsignor Lucyan Bojnowski of New Britain, Connecticut.* Waterbury, CT: Heminway Corp.

Carlson, L. M. (1994). *American eyes: New Asian-American short stories for young adults.* New York: Holt.

Carlson, L. M. (Ed.). (1994). *Cool salsa: Bilingual poems on growing up Latino in the United States.* New York: Holt.

Davis, C. T., & Gates, H. L., Jr. (Eds.). (1985). *The slave's narrative: Texts and contexts.* New York: Oxford University Press.

Debo, A. (1984). *And still the waters run: The betrayal of the five civilized tribes.* Norman, OK: University of Oklahoma Press.

Douglass, F. (1963). *Narrative of the life of Frederick Douglass, an American slave, written by himself.* Garden City, NY: Dolphin Books.

Douglass, P. F. (1939). *The story of German Methodism: Biography of an immigrant soul.* New York: The Methodist Book Concern.

Ehle, J. (1988). *Trail of Tears: The rise and fall of the Cherokee nation.* New York: Anchor Press.

Epstein, M. (1965). *Profiles of eleven: Profiles of eleven men who guided the destiny of an immigrant society and stimulated social consciousness among the American people.* Detroit: Wayne State University Press.

Erdrich, L. (1984). *Love medicine: A novel.* New York: Holt, Rinehart, and Winston.

Foster, F. S. (1979). *Witnessing slavery: The development of ante-bellum slave narratives.* Westport, CT: Greenwood Press.

Galarza, E. (1971). *Barrio boy: The story of a boy's acculturation.* South Bend, IN: Notre Dame University Press.

Gates, H. L. (1987). *The classic slave narratives.* New York: Mentor.

Grant, D. (1968). *The fortunate slave: An illustration of African slavery in the early eighteenth century.* New York: Oxford University Press.

Gross, T. L. (Ed.). (1971). *A nation of nations: Ethnic literature in America.* New York: Free Press.

Grossman, S., & Schur, J. B. (Eds.). (1994). *In a new land: An anthology of immigrant literature.* Lincolnwood, IL: National Textbook Company.

Handlin, M. E., & Layton, M. S. (1983). *Let me hear your voice: Portraits of aging immigrant Jews.* Seattle: University of Washington Press.

Hoffman, E. (1989). *Lost in translation: A life in a new language.* New York: E. P. Dutton.

Hoobler, D., & Hoobler, T. (1995). *The African American family album.* New York: Oxford University Press.

Jastrow, M. (1986). *Looking back: The American dream through immigrant eyes.* New York: Norton.

Josephy, A. M. (1961). *The patriot chiefs: A chronicle of American Indian resistance.* New York: Viking Press.

Josephy, A. M. (Ed.). (1971). *Red power: The American Indians' fight for freedom.* New York: McGraw-Hill.

Karp, A. J. (Ed.). (1976). *Golden door to America: The Jewish immigrant experience.* New York: Viking Press.

Leinwand, G. (Ed.). (1971). *Minorities all.* New York: Washington Square Press.

Meltzer, M. (Ed.). (1995). *Frederick Douglass: In his own words.* New York: Harcourt Brace and Company.

Miller, W. (Ed.). (1972). *A gathering of ghetto writers: Irish, Italian, Jewish, Black, and Puerto Rican.* New York: New York University Press.

Morrison, J., & Zabusky, C. (1980). *American mosaic: The immigrant experience in the words of those who lived it.* New York: Dutton.

Nash, G. B. (1974). *Red, white, and black: The peoples of early America.* Englewood Cliffs, NJ: Prentice-Hall.

Neidle, C. S. (1973). *Great immigrants.* New York: Twayne Publishers.

Neidle, C. S. (1975). *America's immigrant women*. Boston: Twayne Publishers.

Paulsen, G. (1987). *The crossing*. New York: Orchard Books.

Perkins, B., & Perkins, G. (Eds.). (1993). *Kaleidoscope: Stories of the American experience*. New York: Oxford University Press.

Pitt, N. (1986). *Beyond the high white wall*. New York: Charles Scribner's Sons.

Puzo, M. (1969). *The godfather*. New York: Putnam.

Rawick, G. P. (Ed.). (1979). *The American slave: A composite autobiography*. Westport, CT: Greenwood Press.

Ríos, I. (1976). *Victuum*. Ventura, CA: Diana-Etna.

Rodriguez, R. (1981). *Hunger of memory: The education of Richard Rodriguez*. Boston: D. R. Godine.

Rose, P. I. (Ed.). (1972). *Nation of nations: The ethnic experience and the racial crisis*. New York: Random House.

Roth, H. (1965). *Call it sleep: A novel*. New York: Cooper Square Publishers.

Seller, M. (Ed.). (1980). *Immigrant women*. Philadelphia: Temple University Press.

Tan, A. (1989). *The Joy Luck Club*. New York: Putnam.

Tan, A. (1991). *The kitchen god's wife*. New York: Putnam.

Taulbert, C. L. (1989). *Once upon a time when we were colored*. Tulsa, OK: Council Oak Books.

Turner, N. (1861). *Confessions of Nat Turner, leader of the late insurrection in Southampton, Va., as fully and voluntarily made to Thomas C. Gray* (facs. ed.). Salem, NH: Ayer.

van der Beets, R. (1973). *Held captive by Indians: Selected narratives, 1642–1836*. Knoxville, TN: University of Tennessee Press.

Villarreal, J. A. (1970). *Pocho*. Garden City, NY: Anchor Books.

Wheeler, T. C. (Ed.). (1972). *The immigrant experience: The anguish of becoming American*. New York: Penguin Books.

Teaching Multiethnic Issues

Books and Articles

Acuña, R. (1988). *Occupied America: A history of Chicanos* (3rd ed.). New York: Harper & Row.

Alba, R. D. (Ed.). (1988). *Ethnicity and race in the U.S.A.: Toward the twenty-first century*. New York: Routledge.

Allen, J. P., & Turner, E. J. (1988). *We the people: An atlas of America's ethnic diversity*. New York: Macmillan.

Archdeacon, T. J. (1983). *Becoming American: An ethnic history*. New York: The Free Press.

Banks, J. A. (1991). *Teaching strategies for ethnic studies* (5th ed.). Boston: Allyn & Bacon.

Bodnar, J. (1985). *The transplanted: A history of immigrants in urban America*. Bloomington, IN: Indiana University Press.

Butler, J. E., & Walter, J. C. (Eds.). (1991). *Transforming the curriculum: Ethnic studies and women's studies*. Albany: State University of New York Press.

Calloway, C. G. (Ed.). (1988). *New directions in American Indian history*. Norman, OK: University of Oklahoma Press.

Cordasco, F. (1985). *The immigrant woman in North America: An annotated bibliography of selected references*. Metuchen, NJ: Scarecrow Press.

Cordasco, F. (1987). *The new American immigration: Evolving patterns of legal and illegal emigration: A bibliography of selected references.* New York: Garland.

Cordasco, F. (Ed.). (1990). *A dictionary of American immigration history.* Metuchen, NJ: Scarecrow Press.

Dinnerstein, L., Nichols, R. L., & Reimers, D. M. (1990). *Natives and strangers: Blacks, Indians, and immigrants in America* (2nd ed.). New York: Oxford University Press.

Dinnerstein, L., & Reimers, D. M. (1987). *Ethnic Americans: A history of immigration* (3rd ed.). New York: Harper & Row.

Franklin, J. H., & Moss, A. A., Jr. (1988). *From slavery to freedom: A history of Negro Americans* (6th ed.). New York: Knopf.

Gallimore, R., Boggs, J., & Jordan, C. (1974). *Culture, behavior, and education: A study of Hawaiian-Americans.* Beverly Hills, CA: Sage Publications.

Goebel, B. A., & Hall, J. (Eds.). (1995). *Teaching a "new canon"?: Students, teachers, and texts in the college literature classroom.* Urbana, IL: National Council of Teachers of English.

Hamilton, V. (1988). *Anthony Burns: The defeat and triumph of a fugitive slave.* New York: Knopf.

Handlin, O. (1951). *The uprooted: The epic story of the great migrations that made the American people.* New York: Grosset & Dunlap.

Haskins, J. (1987). *Black music in America: A history through its people.* New York: Thomas Y. Crowell.

Hertzberg, A. (1989). *The Jews in America: Four centuries of an uneasy encounter: A history.* New York: Simon & Schuster.

Jones, J. (1986). *Labor of love, labor of sorrow: Black women, work, and the family from slavery to the present.* New York: Vintage Books.

Kim, H-C. (Ed.). (1986). *Dictionary of Asian American history.* New York: Greenwood Press.

Kivisto, P. (Ed.). (1989). *The ethnic enigma: The salience of ethnicity for European-origin ethnic groups.* Philadelphia: The Balch Institute Press.

Knoll, T. (1982). *Becoming Americans: Asian sojourners, immigrants, and refugees in the western United States.* Portland, OR: Coast to Coast Books.

Mindel, C. H., Habenstein, R. W., & Wright, R., Jr. (Eds.). (1988). *Ethnic families in America: Patterns and variations* (3rd ed.). New York: Elsevier.

Mitchell, D. D. K. (1972). *Resource units in Hawaiian culture.* Honolulu: The Kamehameha Schools.

Moquin, W. (Ed.). (1971). *Makers of America* (Vols. 1–10). Chicago: Encyclopedia Britannica Educational Corporation.

Nash, G. B. (1974). *Red, white, and black: The peoples of early America.* Englewood Cliffs, NJ: Prentice-Hall.

Oliver, E. I. (1994). *Crossing the mainstream: Multicultural perspectives in teaching literature.* Urbana, IL: National Council of Teachers of English.

Reimers, D. M. (1985). *Still the golden door: The third world comes to America.* New York: Columbia University Press.

Rochman, H. (1993). *Against borders: Promoting books for a multicultural world.* Chicago: American Library Association.

Rosenberg, M. B. (1986). *Making a new home in America.* New York: Lothrop, Lee, and Shepard Books.

Seller, M. (1980). *Immigrant women*. Philadelphia: Temple University Press.

Sleeter, C. E. (Ed.). (1991). *Empowerment through multicultural education*. Albany: State University of New York Press.

Sleeter, C. E., & Grant, C. A. (1988). *Making choices for multicultural education: Five approaches to race, class, and gender*. Columbus, OH: Merrill Publishing Company.

Stotsky, S. (1995). Guidelines for selecting European ethnic literature for interdisciplinary courses. *English Leadership Quarterly, 17*(1), 1–6.

Takaki, R. (1989). *Strangers from a different shore: A history of Asian Americans*. Boston: Little, Brown.

Wilson, A. (1987). *"Mixed race" children: A study of identity*. Boston: Allen & Unwin.

Journal

Multicultural Leader, Educational Materials and Services Center, 144 Railroad Ave., Suite 107, Edmonds, WA 98020

Organizations and Committees

Assembly on Alternatives for English Language Arts Instruction for Students with Diverse Academic Needs of the National Council of Teachers of English

NCTE Advisory Committee of People of Color

NCTE Commission on Educators of Color (subcommittee of the Conference on English Education)

NCTE Commission on Teacher Education for Teachers of Urban, Rural, and Suburban Students of Color (subcommittee of the Conference on English Education)

NCTE Commission on Urban Schools (subcommittee of the Conference on English Leadership)

NCTE Committee on Racism and Bias in the Teaching of English

NCTE Committee on Teaching about Genocide and Intolerance

NCTE Task Force on Involving People of Color in the Council

NCTE/SLATE Steering Committee on Social and Political Concerns

Portfolios

Books

Belanoff, P., & Dickson, M. (Eds.). (1991). *Portfolios: Process and product*. Portsmouth, NH: Boynton/Cook Publishers.

Black, L., Daiker, D. A., Sommers, J., & Stygall, G. (1994). *New directions in portfolio assessment: Reflective practice, critical theory, and large-scale scoring*. Portsmouth, NH: Boynton/Cook Publishers.

Gill, K. (Ed.). (1993). *Process and portfolios in writing instruction*. Classroom Practices in Teaching English, Volume 26. Urbana, IL: National Council of Teachers of English.

Gomez, M. L., Graue, M. E., & Bloch, M. N. (1991). Reassessing portfolio assessment: Rhetoric and reality. *Language Arts, 68*(8), 620–628.

Hamp-Lyons, L., & Condon, W. (1993). Questioning assumptions about portfolio-based assessment. *College Composition and Communication, 44*(2), 176–190.

Hewitt, G. (1995). *A portfolio primer: Teaching, collecting, and assessing student writing*. Portsmouth, NH: Heinemann.

Porter, C., & Cleland, J. (1995). *The portfolio as a learning strategy.* Portsmouth, NH: Boynton/Cook Publishers.

Rogers, T., & Soter, A. (Eds.). (1994, Spring/Summer). *Redefining the boundaries of portfolio assessment.* Special issue of *Ohio Journal of the English Language Arts, 35*(1).

Smith, M. A., & Ylvisaker, M. (Eds.). (1993). *Teachers' voices: Portfolios in the classroom.* Berkeley, CA: National Writing Project.

Tierney, R., Carter, M., & Desai, L. (1991). *Portfolio assessment in the reading-writing classroom.* Norwood, MA: Christopher-Gordon Publishers.

Wolf, D., Bixby, J., Glen, J., & Gardner, G. (1991). To use their minds well: Investigating new forms of assessment. In L. Darling-Hammond (Ed.), *Review of Research in Education* (pp. 31–74). Washington, D. C.: American Educational Research Association.

Yancey, K. B. (Ed.). (1992). *Portfolios in the writing classroom: An introduction.* Urbana, IL: National Council of Teachers of English.

Using the Internet

Books

Cumming, J., & Sayers, D. (1995). *Brave new schools: Challenging cultural illiteracy through global learning networks.* New York: St. Martin's Press.

Engst, A. C. (1994). *Internet starter kit for Macintosh* (2nd ed.). Indianapolis, IN: Hayden Books.

Fraase, M. (1993). *The Mac Internet tour guide: Cruising the Internet the easy way.* Chapel Hill, NC: Ventana Press.

Fraase, M. (1994). *The Windows Internet tour guide: Cruising the Internet the easy way.* Chapel Hill, NC: Ventana Press.

Frey, D., & Adams, R. (1994). *!%@:: A directory of electronic mail addressing and networks* (4th ed.). Sebastopol, CA: O'Reilly & Associates.

Harris, J. (1994). *Way of the ferret: Finding educational resources on the Internet.* Eugene, OR: ISTE.

Krol, E. (1993). *The whole Internet: User's guide and catalog.* Sebastopol, CA: O'Reilly & Associates.

Pierce, J. W., Blomeyer, R., & Roberts, T. M. (1995). Surfing the Internet: A whale of an information source for educational researchers. *Educational Researcher, 24*(5), 25–26.

Using Computer Technology

Books, Chapters, and Articles

Brooks, J. G., & Brooks, M. G. (1993). *In search of understanding: The case for constructivist classrooms.* Alexandria, VA: Association for Supervision and Curriculum Development.

Bruce, B., Peyton, J. K., & Batson, T. (Eds.). (1993). *Network-based classrooms: Promises and realities.* Cambridge: Cambridge University Press.

Franklin, S. (Ed.). (1991). *Writing & technology: Ideas that work–the best of the Writing Notebook* (Vol. 2). Eugene, OR: Visions for Learning.

Handa, C. (Ed.). (1990). *Computers and community: Teaching composition in the twenty-first century.* Portsmouth, NH: Boynton/Cook Publishers.

Handler, M., Dana, A., & Moore, J. (1995). *Hypermedia as a student tool: A guide for teachers.* Englewood, CO: Libraries Unlimited/Teachers Ideas Press.

Hawisher, G., & LeBlanc, P. (Eds.). (1992). *Re-imagining computers and composition: Teaching and research in the virtual age.* Portsmouth, NH: Boynton/Cook Publishers.

Holmes, K., & Rawitsch, D. (1993). *Evaluating technology-based instructional programs.* Denton, TX: Texas Center for Educational Technology.

Honey, M., & Henriquez, A. (1993). *Telecommunications and K–12 educators: Findings from a national survey.* New York: Center for Technology in Education. Bank Street College of Education.

Howie, S. H. (1989). *Reading, writing, and computers: Planning for integration.* Boston: Allyn & Bacon.

Katzer, S., & Crnkovich, C. A. (1991). *From scribblers to scribes: Young writers use the computer.* Englewood, CO: Teachers Ideas Press.

Kearsley, G., & Lynch, W. (1994). *Educational technology: Leadership perspectives.* Englewood Cliffs, NJ: Educational Technology Publications.

Keefe, J. W., & Walberg, H. J. (Eds.). (1992). *Teaching for thinking.* Reston, VA: National Association of Secondary School Principals.

Lea, M. (Ed.). (1992). *Contexts of computer-mediated communication.* New York: Wheatsheaf.

LeBlanc, P. (1993). *Writing teachers writing software: Creating our place in the electronic age.* Urbana, IL: National Council of Teachers of English.

Malle, M. (1994). *Teaching for inclusion* (2nd ed.). Boston: Allyn & Bacon.

Means, B. (Ed.). (1994). *Technology and education reform: The reality behind the promise.* San Francisco: Jossey-Bass.

Monroe, R. (1993). *Writing and thinking with computers: A practical guide and progressive approach.* Urbana, IL: National Council of Teachers of English.

Nardi, B. A. (Ed.). (1996). *Context and consciousness: Activity theory and human–computer interaction.* Cambridge, MA: MIT Press.

Perkins, D. N., Schwartz, J. L., West, M. M., & Wiske, M. S. (Eds.). (1995). *Software goes to school: Teaching for understanding with new technologies.* New York: Oxford University Press.

Selfe, C. (1989). *Creating a computer-supported writing facility: A blueprint for action.* Houghton, MI: Computers & Composition, Michigan Technology University.

Thornburg, D. (1992). *Edutrends 2010: Restructuring, technology, and the future of education.* Mountain View, CA: Starsong Publications.

Turner, S., & Land, M. (1994). *Hypercard: A tool for learning.* Belmont, CA: Wadsworth Publishing Company.

Journals

Computers and Composition, Gail Hawisher, University of Illinois

Computers in Human Behavior, Elsevier Science Ltd., Tarry Town, NY

Human-Computer Interaction, Lawrence Erlbaum Associates

Journal of Research on Computing in Education, International Society for Technology in Education, Houston, TX

Library Software Review, Sage Publications

Organizations and Committees

NCTE Assembly on Computers in English

NCTE Commission on Media

NCTE Committee on Computers in Composition and Communication (subcommittee of the Conference on College Composition and Communication)

NCTE Committee on Information Literacy
NCTE Committee on Instructional Technology

Conferences, Collaboration, and Writing Groups

Books, Chapters, and Articles

Anson, C. (Ed.). (1989). *Writing and response: Theory, practice, and research.* Urbana, IL: National Council of Teachers of English.

Brooke, R., Mirtz, R., & Evans, R. (1994). *Small groups in writing workshops: Invitations to a writer's life.* Urbana, IL: National Council of Teachers of English.

Brubacher, M., Payne, R., & Rickett, K. (Eds.). (1990). *Perspectives on small group learning: Theory and practice.* Ontario, Canada: Rubicon.

Cohen, E. G. (1994). *Designing groupwork: Strategies for the heterogeneous classroom* (2nd ed.). New York: Teachers College Press.

Davidson, N., & Worsham, T. (Eds.). (1992). *Enhancing thinking through cooperative learning.* New York: Teachers College Press.

Dawe, C. W., & Dornan, E. A. (1987). *One to one: Resources for conference centered writing* (3rd ed.). Portsmouth, NH: Boynton/Cook Publishers.

DiPardo, A., & Freedman, S. W. (1988). Peer response groups in the writing classroom: Theoretic foundations and new directions. *Review of Educational Research, 58*(2), 119–149.

Dressman, M. (1993). Lionizing lone wolves: The cultural romantics of literacy workshops. *Curriculum Inquiry, 23:* 245–263.

Dyson, A. H. (Ed.). (1989). *Collaboration through writing and reading: Exploring possibilities.* Urbana, IL: National Council of Teachers of English.

Flynn, T., & King, M. (Eds.). (1993). *Dynamics of the writing conference: Social and cognitive interactions.* Urbana, IL: National Council of Teachers of English.

Gere, A. R. (1987). *Writing groups: History, theory, and implications.* Carbondale, IL: Southern Illinois University Press.

Golub, J. (Ed.). (1980). *Focus on collaborative learning: Classroom practices in teaching English.* Urbana, IL: National Council of Teachers of English.

Golub, J. (1994). *Activities for an interactive classroom.* Urbana, IL: National Council of Teachers of English.

Harris, M. (1986). *Teaching one to one: The writing conference.* Urbana, IL: National Council of Teachers of English.

Johnson, D., Johnson, R., & Holubec, E. (1990). *Circles of learning: Cooperation in the classroom* (3rd ed.). Edinah, MN: Interaction Book Company.

Kutz, E., & Roskelly, H. (1991). *An unquiet pedagogy: Transforming practice in the English classroom.* Portsmouth, NH: Heinemann.

Newkirk, T. (1995). The writing conference as performance. *Research in the Teaching of English, 29*(2), 193–215.

Peterson, P., Wilkinson, L., & Hallinan, M. (Eds.). (1984). *The social context of instruction: Group organization and group processes.* New York: Academic Press.

Rubin, D. L., & Dodd, W. M. (1987). *Talking into writing: Exercises for basic writers.* Urbana, IL: ERIC Clearinghouse on Reading and Communication Skills and National Council of Teachers of English.

Sharan, Y., & Sharan, S. (1992). *Expanding cooperative learning through group investigation.* New York: Teachers College Press.

Smagorinsky, P. (1991). The aware audience: Role-playing peer-response groups. *English Journal, 80*(5), 35–40.

Smagorinsky, P., & Fly, P. K. (1994). A new perspective on why small groups do and don't work. *English Journal, 83*(3), 54–58.

Spear, K. (1987). *Sharing writing: Peer response groups in English classes.* Portsmouth, NH: Boynton/Cook Publishers.

Spear, K. (1993). *Peer response groups in action: Writing together in secondary schools.* Portsmouth, NH: Boynton/Cook Publishers.

Sperling, M. (1990). I want to talk to each of you: Collaboration and the teacher-student writing conference. *Research in the Teaching of English, 24*(3), 279–321.

Sperling, M. (1991). Dialogues of deliberation: Conversation in the teacher-student writing conference. *Written Communication, 8*(2), 131–162.

Tobin, L. (1993). *Writing relationships: What really happens in the composition class.* Portsmouth, NH: Heinemann.

Willinsky, J. (1990). *The new literacy: Redefining reading and writing in schools.* New York: Routledge.

Video

Cohen, E. G. (1994). *Status treatments for the classroom.* New York: Teachers College Press.

Journal

Small Group Research, Sage Publications

Committee

NCTE Committee on Alternatives to Grading Student Writing

GLOSSARY

This glossary is intended to provide a brief introduction to some terms used in this book. If readers wish for more detailed information, they should consult the lists of resources located at the end of each chapter.

Cooperative Learning: Cooperative learning stresses the social aspects of learning. Advocates of cooperative learning criticize conventional school structure and assessment in which students are isolated for instruction and evaluation and compete with one another for grades. Cooperative learning usually involves small groups of students working together towards a common end. Rather than competing with one another for a grade, they try to pool their resources to develop a group product. Students both learn from and teach one another under such arrangements.

Cooperative learning does not simply "work" by putting students together. There are no universal formulas concerning group size, group composition, task structure, incentive structure, or other aspects of group formation and process. In general, in cooperative learning situations each participant seeks to help others learn and grow, and the group members share a common goal. The process through which a group functions towards this end varies from situation to situation, and is a function of the processes that govern a class as a whole. In other words, a class in which a teacher primarily lectures and grades according to a competitive curve is not likely to have a smooth transition to a cooperative small-group setting, a setting that requires learners to discuss complex, open-ended problems and issues to achieve collaborative, mutual understanding. A cooperative learning environment needs to be fostered through collaborative work in both whole-class and small-group discussions and activities.

Grammar: In *Grammar for Teachers,* Constance Weaver points out that the term "grammar" refers to many different things. Among them are:

1. "Grammar" is synonymous with syntax, and thus refers to aspects of sentence structure.
2. "Grammar" is synonymous with "usage"; thus, "good grammar" refers to standard usage of English.

3. In linguistics, a "grammar" describes the syntactic structure of a language.
4. In psycholinguistics, a "grammar" describes the processes by which sentences are produced and comprehended.
5. "Grammar" is a text book used for teaching the first four notions of grammar.

"Traditional grammar instruction" refers to instruction in the parts of speech independent of the social uses of language. By most accounts, traditional grammar instruction is among the most widely practiced method of teaching both language usage and writing in American schools. According to Weaver, "as long ago as 1936, the Curriculum Commission of the National Council of Teachers of English recommended that 'all teaching of grammar separate from the manipulation of sentences be discontinued . . . since every scientific attempt to prove that knowledge of grammar is useful has failed . . . '" (p. 5). Both Braddock, Lloyd-Jones, and Schoer's *Research in Written Composition* (which reviewed writing research from 1943–1963) and Hillocks's *Research on Written Composition* (which reviewed writing research from 1963–1983) emphatically support this conclusion.

Multiple Intelligences: Howard Gardner developed his theory of multiple intelligences through studies of neurology and cultural history. He believes that people have seven "intelligences," which involve both problem solving and problem finding: *linguistic* intelligence, which is the ability to use language with facility; *logical/mathematical* intelligence, which allows one to compute numbers or string together chains of logic; *musical* intelligence, which allows a person to create or appreciate configurations of sound in an effective way; *spatial* intelligence, through which one configures space for a desired effect; *bodily/kinesthetic* intelligence, which is the intelligent use of the body; *interpersonal* intelligence, through which people understand one another; and *intrapersonal* intelligence, through which people understand themselves. The implications of his theory for English/language arts classes are that productivity and assessment should not be confined to narrow areas of intelligence, such as the individual production of analytic essays, but should involve drama, art, music, collaboration, introspection, and other types of performances as well.

Portfolio: The idea of a portfolio is borrowed from the art world, where artists keep a selection of their best, most representative work to show to others for evaluation. Assessing language arts students through portfolios is a response to conventional evaluation in which a student receives a grade for every assignment done, and in which a final grade is determined through a computation of the average of all scores. By using conventional evaluation, teachers value the product of student work at the expense of the process behind its production, and also assume that the grade a student ultimately receives for a marking period is the sum total of all efforts. Portfolio approaches assume that students make mistakes, learn through errors, require time to develop skills, and otherwise are involved in a learning process as they work towards the completion of a product. In a portfolio approach, grading each and every step in the learning process can be punitive and ultimately provides a false picture of a student's learning. Students are instead evaluated on a smaller set of finished products, with the steps taken along the way evaluated and responded to but not always officially graded. Often a portfolio will include not only finished products, but the series of drafts that the student generated in order to arrive at the final version. All finished products are not necessarily included; students may make selections from among portfolio items rather than submitting them all, allowing students opportunities to experiment with topics and genres without the fear of evaluative repercussions. Finally, portfolio approaches stress the learner's reflection and self-evaluation. Drafts, outlines, and other efforts undertaken in the process of writing often serve as opportunities for students to reflect on how they learn, with this reflection coming through writing (perhaps in a journal), through conferences with the teacher and/or other students, or through another medium.

Process Approaches to Teaching Writing: References to "the writing process" are now common among English teachers. The "process movement" began as a response to instruction that focused on written products. Product-oriented instruction typically focused on form at both the text and sentence levels. The form of a text was emphasized by showing students model essays of a particular genre such as the five-paragraph theme, having them label its parts, and then asking them to imitate these parts in essays of their own. Sentence level form was a focus of traditional grammar instruction in which students learned to label the parts of speech and parse sentences written by someone else, and were then instructed to follow the grammatical rules they'd studied in their own writing.

Process-oriented approaches are more concerned with the generation of content, with aspects of form coming later during consideration of the finished product's communicative purpose. Often teachers refer to "the writing process" as a series of stages progressing from prewriting to drafting to revising to editing to completion, with feedback from peers and/or teachers taking place throughout the process. At times writing instruction under the "process" banner is reduced to a linear progression through these stages. Many teachers feel the process ought to be more recursive, with each "stage" taking place during all others. There is disagreement over whether there is a single writing process that students can learn to guide all of their writing, or whether different tasks and communities require attention to specific features, thus necessitating an understanding of a possibly infinite variety of writing processes.

Reader-Response Theory: Reader-response theory regards reading as a constructive process. From this perspective a written text does not have an inherent meaning, but takes on meaning through a reader's response to it. A reader reads a text somewhat in the same way that a musician "reads" a musical score: The notes provide a guide that the musician interprets according to a personal vision. Excessive improvisation is worthy in its own way, but does not constitute a "reading" of the written score. In the same manner, a reader of a written text needs to follow the words but imputes personal meaning to them.

In *A Teacher's Introduction to Reader-Response Theories*, Richard Beach describes five types of influences on a reader's construction of meaning for the words of a written text:

Text-based: The written text itself is written according to codes. At times these are obvious, such as the use of subheads in an academic article; at times they are subtle, such as the use of cultural references, e.g., Faulkner's title *Absalom, Absalom!*, to signify relationships within a literary work. The manner in which a reader recognizes these textual codes and constructs a meaning for them determines the "meaning" that a text will have for him or her.

Psychological: Readers rely on frameworks known as "scripts" or "schemata" to inform their reading. These scripts might come from knowledge of genres: A scientist knows how a research report is structured and uses that knowledge to locate information quickly. A script might also come from personal experience: people who have experienced absurdity will use that knowledge to inform their understanding of the characters in novels by Kurt Vonnegut, Jr.

Experiential: Every reader brings personal experiences to a reading that affect the ways in which meaning is constructed. These experiences may affect meaning construction for fiction and nonfiction as well. In fiction, a reader may have experienced ostracism in such a way as to create sympathy for Hester Prynne and antipathy towards the townspeople in *The Scarlet Letter.* In nonfiction, a reader may read a history book and develop sympathies based on personal experiences parallel to those of historical figures.

Social: The social environment of learning can affect how readers respond to literature. A classroom that regards literature as a puzzle to be solved according to a single formula will encourage readers to respond in one way; a class in which students keep reading logs, talk about how they feel about the characters, and are encouraged to make personal connections to characters will encourage readers to respond in another.

Cultural: Readers' cultural backgrounds can affect their response to literature. This phenomenon helps explain why many African American readers have a negative reaction to Twain's *Huckleberry Finn,* or why a woman reader might feel empty or angry reading fiction in which female characters serve primarily as props.

In practice, all five of these factors contribute to a reader's response. If I read Faulkner's *As I Lay Dying,* I recognize Faulkner's use of spiral form and multiple narrators (text-based); use my schematic knowledge of journey myths (psychological); draw on personal knowledge of avarice to recognize Anse's motives (experiential); read according to prevailing values, such as the New Critical values of the college classes I attended or the affective orientation of an adult reading club (social); and draw on cultural knowledge, such as shared references for the Biblical images of fire and water (cultural). Often, however, theorists and teachers believe that one of these approaches ought to prevail at the expense of others.

Reading/Writing Workshops: Workshops are activity-oriented classrooms that involve a great deal of student choice and autonomy in directing their learning. A writing workshop is devoted entirely to writing, often invoking Dewey's notions of "discovery learning" and "learning by doing" to justify the method. Students typically identify their own writing goals in conferences with the teacher, and then student and teacher set up a personal curriculum that will lead to the achievement of those goals. Students' grades are determined by the degree to which they meet their own goals. Students may use class time to work on any writing of their choice. The teacher's role is to oversee student production, meet frequently with each student in conferences, maintain records of progress, make decisions about whether group instruction in particular areas is necessary and provide that instruction in brief "mini-lessons," provide a formal beginning and ending to each class in whole group meetings where students can share thoughts and writing, and otherwise facilitate students' progress toward their goals. Teachers in such classes often write along with their students and share their writing during group sharing times.

Scaffolding: The metaphor of an "instructional scaffold" comes from Jerome Bruner's effort to translate Vygotsky's developmental psychology into teaching principles. A scaffold refers to the support a teacher provides for students during the early stages of learning a specific skill. Ideally, students will receive explicit support early in a learning process and have that support gradually withdrawn as they take greater responsibility for learning. Teachers scaffold learning by clearly articulating goals and providing students with an understanding of how particular tools (e.g., writing and reading strategies) can help them achieve the stated goals. Often students move from teacher-supported whole group settings to small groups where they support one another's development without the teacher's direct intervention, and finally move toward independent performance.

Some have criticized this metaphor for being too top-down, and have argued in the manner of Dewey that learning is a *joint activity* between teachers and learners that requires negotiation and reconstruction of the goals and uses of learning tools. A scaffold, therefore, needs to be co-constructed by teachers and students. Others have criticized the idea of scaffolding because it places teachers in the directive role of determining the learning goals students ought to have and the processes through which they ought to achieve them. Such approaches are not sufficiently "student-centered" to these critics, and can involve cultural bias when members of cultural minorities are taught that their own ways of communicating and purposes for learning are not valued by schools.

Student- and Teacher-Centered Instruction: Most educational publications today favor "student-centered" (aka "progressive" or "transformative") teaching, often in contrast with what is called "teacher-centered" (aka "traditional," "mimetic," or "academic") teaching. The person at the "center" of teaching decides what content and processes are learned, and how, when, and under what arrangement that learning takes place. Larry Cuban, in *How Teachers Taught*, defines the two extremes as follows:

Student-Centered Instruction: Students talk at least as much as the teacher; instruction usually takes place individually or in small groups; students help choose and organize the course content; students help determine the classroom rules; classrooms include a variety of learning stations to suit different student interests—these stations are available at least half the time; furniture (and thus student configurations) is realigned frequently.

Teacher-Centered Instruction: Teacher talk exceeds student talk; whole class instruction predominates, with students usually seated in rows facing the teacher in front; the teacher determines the content and process of study; the teacher relies on a textbook for decision making.

In actual practice, these approaches represent extremes on a continuum, with most teachers falling somewhere in between the two as what Cuban calls "hybrids."

Teacher-Research: Teacher-research (aka "action research") refers to research conducted by teachers on their own teaching. Historically, teacher-research has had low status among educational researchers because university researchers have controlled the terms of discussions about research. Recently teacher-research has gained greater credibility because many have begun to argue that it be viewed and evaluated on its own terms rather than on those preferred by university researchers. University researchers have historically valued research that can be "replicated"; that is, research where the findings are the same no matter where the research is conducted. Teacher-research now emphasizes that the most valuable research findings that teachers can achieve are those derived from a study of their own teaching. The particular configuration of teacher, students, school, community, state, and others involved in a teaching-learning relationship provides a specific context that is often poorly informed by research conducted at other sites. Teacher-research is valuable precisely because it *cannot* be replicated; rather it informs specific situations. Teachers who study their own classes can enrich their practice through a greater understanding of the consequences of the particular ways in which they structure their activity with students. According to Cochran-Smith and Lytle in *Inside/Outside*, teacher-research can come in four forms: teacher journals, oral inquiry, classroom studies, and essays.

A second focus of teacher-research is the study of students outside school. Rather than studying classroom processes, these teacher-researchers study students in their homes and communities to try to understand their cultural backgrounds. This knowledge of student life in turn informs classroom practice as a teacher tries to conduct the class so that all learners have equal opportunities to succeed.

Tracking: Tracking refers to efforts to divide students up into homogeneous groups for instruction. Ideally, a "track" will place students of similar performance ability or aptitude together so that a teacher can tailor instruction specifically to each group's needs. Schools often develop three tracks: a top track known as "honors," "high ability," or perhaps a neutral term (such as a color); a middle track known as "regular," "average," or a neutral term; and a low track known as "basic," "essential," "low-ability," or a neutral term. Proponents of tracking argue that such arrangements do not penalize especially high-achieving students by placing them in classes in which instruction is aimed at less able students; similarly, low-achieving students can have instruction geared to an appropriate pace so that they are not left behind by classes designed for more adept students.

Critics of tracking argue that the placement of students is a matter of perception that may underestimate or ignore their various abilities and intelligences. Additionally, tracking can become a self-fulfilling prophecy, that is, a student placed in a track will perform according to the expectations of that track regardless of ability. Tracking is often seen as racist since minority students disproportionally make up the ranks of low tracks and are similarly absent from high tracks. Tracking is criticized for sorting students according to behavior rather than academic performance; students who are "trouble" in school frequently get assigned to low-track classes, creating difficult learning and teaching challenges for the classroom. Finally, tracking can beget a "rich-get-richer" condition within a school; that is, students who get placed in higher tracks early achieve at an accelerated pace and make it unlikely for a student in a lower track to "move up" because of the ever-increasing distance in content and process knowledge.

Writing Across the Curriculum: Proponents of Writing Across the Curriculum (WAC) argue that students should engage in extended writing in all subject areas, even those in which writing has not historically been valued for communication. Advocates argue that through such an arrangement students would engage in extended thought across the curriculum, rather than taking short answer, multiple choice, and true/false tests in content areas. Critics argue that (1) students do not easily transfer writing skills from one genre and discipline to another, thereby making it essential that teachers in all subject areas be knowledgeable writing teachers if WAC programs are to succeed; (2) teachers in all subject areas do not receive training in writing instruction, nor are they usually experienced writers themselves, therefore making WAC goals unlikely to be realized; and (3) writing, while historically the privileged medium in English classes, is not the primary symbol system of other disciplines, therefore making it questionable whether it should be imposed across the curriculum.

Writing to Learn: According to this view, writing is a process through which a learner develops new thoughts at the point of utterance. This view values writing as a tool for developing thought and is often contrasted with conceptions of writing in which only the final product is considered. This view also challenges the belief that writing is a representation of thought, in that thought changes through the use of writing. Often, those who subscribe to a writing-to-learn perspective value journals, freewrites, and other informal, ungraded writing in which people are encouraged to explore topics, ideas, and feelings. Writing-to-Learn movements have been challenged by those who hold that writing is one of many tools through which students may learn during the process of production. From this perspective, writing is one of a variety of tools—including art, dance, and other media—through which students may learn during the process of composition. From this view, writing is *potentially* a tool of great importance to some students, but is not the optimal tool for all. Such critics view *composing* across the curriculum as a more appropriate goal, with the tool of composition varying from student to student and discipline to discipline.

Young Adult Literature: Young Adult Literature (YAL), or Adolescent Literature, is literature (usually novels) in which the protagonist is a young teen. Proponents of YAL believe that the traditional literary canon offers young teenagers little to personally relate to because it does not address the issues that face modern teens and because it rarely emphasizes the experiences faced developmentally by young teens. Proponents argue that students benefit more from reading contemporary books about people their own age than from reading books regarded as classics by adults. Critics argue that most contemporary literature is of lesser literary quality than classic texts and that a curriculum should emphasize long-term quality over short-term interest.

AUTHOR

Peter Smagorinsky taught English in Chicago area high schools from 1976 through 1990 before moving to the University of Oklahoma, where he is now associate professor of English education. He holds degrees from Kenyon College (B.A.) and the University of Chicago (M.A.T., Ph.D.). His teaching experiences have led him to study the effects of different types of instruction on students' writing processes, the relationship between the processes involved in teacher-led and small-group discussions of literature, multimedia composing across the high school curriculum, and methods of teaching preservice English teachers. Publications from these studies have appeared in *American Journal of Education, Communication Education, English Education, English Journal, JRB: A Journal of Literacy, Reading & Writing Quarterly, Research in the Teaching of English, Review of Educational Research, Voices from the Middle, Written Communication*, and other journals; recent books include co-authorship of *The Language of Interpretation* and *How English Teachers Get Taught*, both from NCTE, and the edited volume *Speaking about Writing*. He is currently on the executive board of the Oklahoma Council of Teachers of English, is acting chair of NCTE's Standing Committee on Research, and co-chairs NCTE's Assembly on Research. He has also served as a consultant on standards projects sponsored by the National Board for Professional Teaching Standards and the U.S. Department of Education.

Other Books from NCTE Related to English Language Arts Content Standards

Standards for the English Language Arts

From the National Council of Teachers of English and the International Reading Association

What should English language arts students know and be able to do? This book—the culmination of more than three years of intense research and discussion among members of the English language arts teaching community, parents, and policymakers—answers this question by presenting standards that encompass the use of print, oral, and visual language and addresses six inter-related English language arts: reading, writing, speaking, listening, viewing, and visually representing. *Standards for the English Language Arts* starts by examining the rationale for standard setting—why NCTE and IRA believe defining standards is important and what we hope to accomplish by doing so. The book then explores the assumptions that underlie the standards, defines and elaborates each standard individually, and provides real-life classroom vignettes in which readers can glimpse standards in practice. Designed to complement state and local standards efforts, this document will help educators prepare *all* K–12 students for the literacy demands of the twenty-first century. 1996. Grades K–12. ISBN 0-8141-4676-7.
Stock No. 46767-4025
$18.00 nonmembers, $13.00 NCTE members

Standards Consensus Series

Books in this series serve as useful guides for K–12 teachers who are striving to align lively, classroom-tested practices with standards. A survey of local, state, and national documents revealed a broad consensus in the key topics most frequently addressed in standards; clearly local conditions may vary, but English language arts teachers across the country face many common challenges as they help students meet higher literacy standards. These first releases in the Standards Consensus Series draw on these common threads and bring together the best teaching ideas from prior NCTE publications in topical books with practical, everyday applications in the classroom. Among the titles available:

Teaching the Writing Process in High School (ISBN 0-8141-5286-4)
Stock No. 52864-4025
$12.95 nonmembers, $9.95 NCTE members

Teaching Literature in High School: The Novel (ISBN 0-8141-5282-1)
Stock No. 52821-4025
$12.95 nonmembers, $9.95 NCTE members

Teaching Literature in Middle School: Fiction (ISBN 0-8141-5285-6)
Stock No. 52856-4025
$12.95 nonmembers; $9.95 NCTE members

Motivating Writing in Middle School (ISBN 0-8141-5287-2)
Stock No. 52872-4025
$12.95 nonmembers, $9.95 NCTE members

Additional Titles in the Standards in Practice Series

Standards in Practice, Grades K–2 by Linda K. Crafton (ISBN 0-8141-4691-0)
   Stock No. 46910-4025
   $15.95 nonmembers, $11.95 NCTE members

Standards in Practice, Grades 3–5 by Martha Sierra-Perry (ISBN 0-8141-4693-7)
   Stock No. 46937-4025
   $15.95 nonmembers, $11.95 NCTE members

Standards in Practice, Grades 6–8 by Jeffrey D. Wilhelm (ISBN 0-8141-4694-5)
   Stock No. 46945-4025
   $15.95 nonmembers, $11.95 NCTE members

Ordering Information

Any of the useful resources described above can be ordered from the National Council of Teachers of English by phoning 1-800-369-6283; by faxing your order to 1-217-328-9645; by e-mailing your order request to <orders@ncte.org>; or by sending your order to NCTE Order Fulfillment, 1111 W. Kenyon Road, Urbana, IL 61801-1096.

To preview these resources, visit the NCTE home page at <http://www.ncte.org>.